Sara's Paintings and Poetry

Sara Lou Coyle

Copyright © 2018 Sara Lou Coyle

All rights reserved.

ISBN: **17121139389**
ISBN-13: **978-1721139385**

DEDICATION

Dedicated to the many artists whose watercolor workshops I attended,
including Rex Brandt, Tom Fong and Joe Cibere.
And also to the writing teachers who inspired me-
Lillian Rodich, Roberta Gillerman, and Virginia Watts
Thank you for opening my eyes to the world.

ACKNOWLEDGMENT

I am grateful to Jessica Lesko for putting my books together with her amazing computer skills!

Cover Painting: Yosemite

Wanna ride?
Take a ride with Sara on her travels near and far.

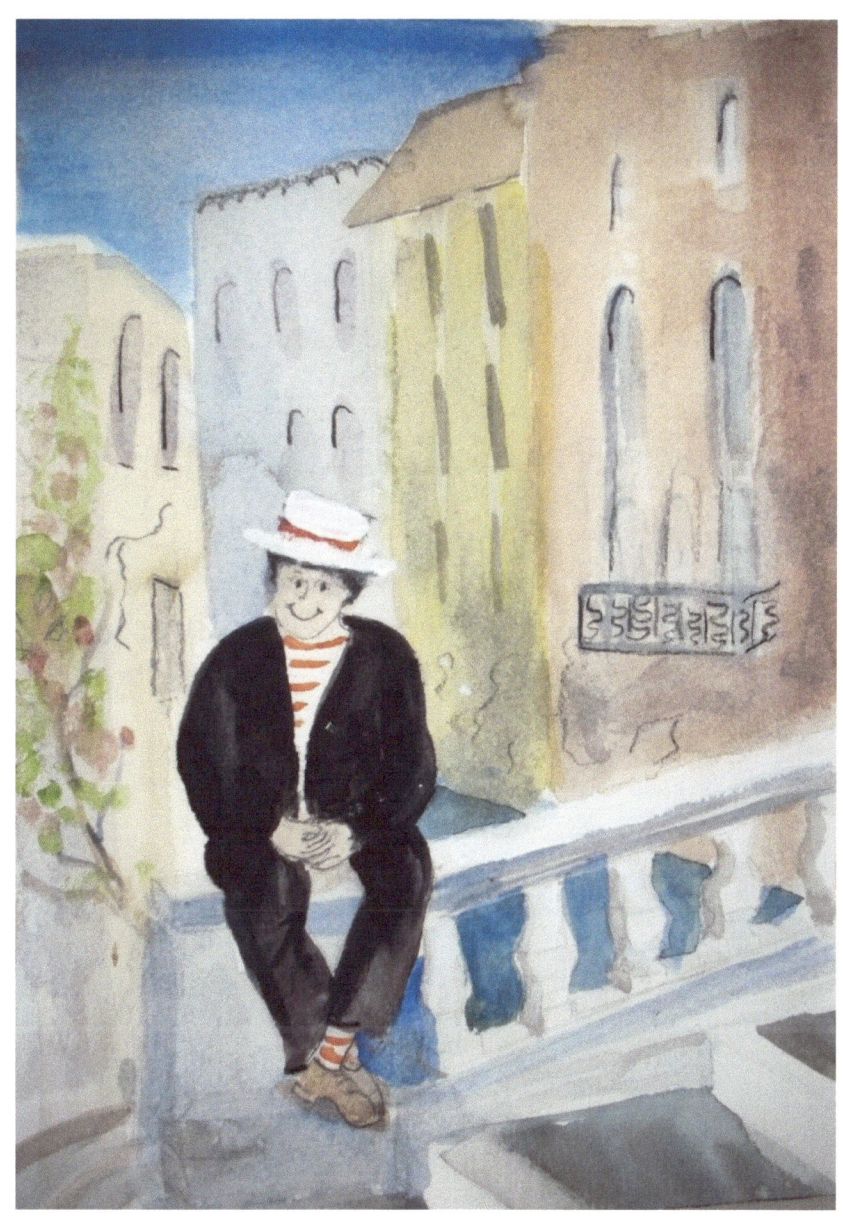

Venice Gondolier

TRAVELS- NEAR AND FAR

I traveled with my sister, daughter and many friends.
My husband, Frank, liked to stay home with our dog- but
he always said to me, "Whatever you do, have fun!"
And I did. Thank you Frank..

The Sky Above

Wherever you go

in this world

the sky is there

above your head

bright blue to grey

clouds changing shapes

rain splashing rainbows

snow fluttering down

sunsets ending our day

stars and the moon lighting our way

beauty above us

always changing

day in and day out

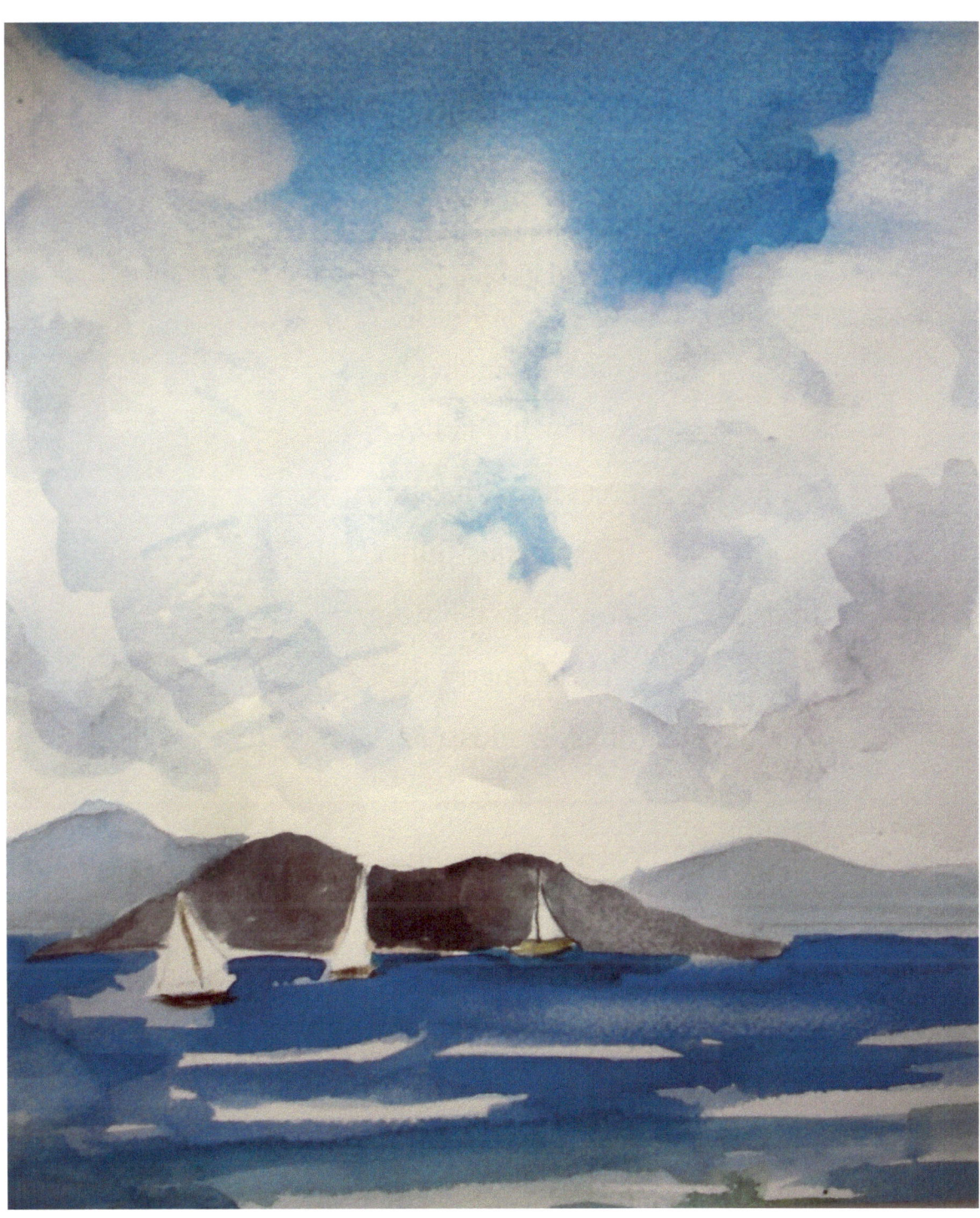

Lake Balboa

When March comes,
Lake Balboa
is surrounded by
dancing ladies,
dressed in pink tutus.
The petals flutter
down into the water.
These cherry trees
blow blossoms
in the air
adding beauty,
reflected in the lake.

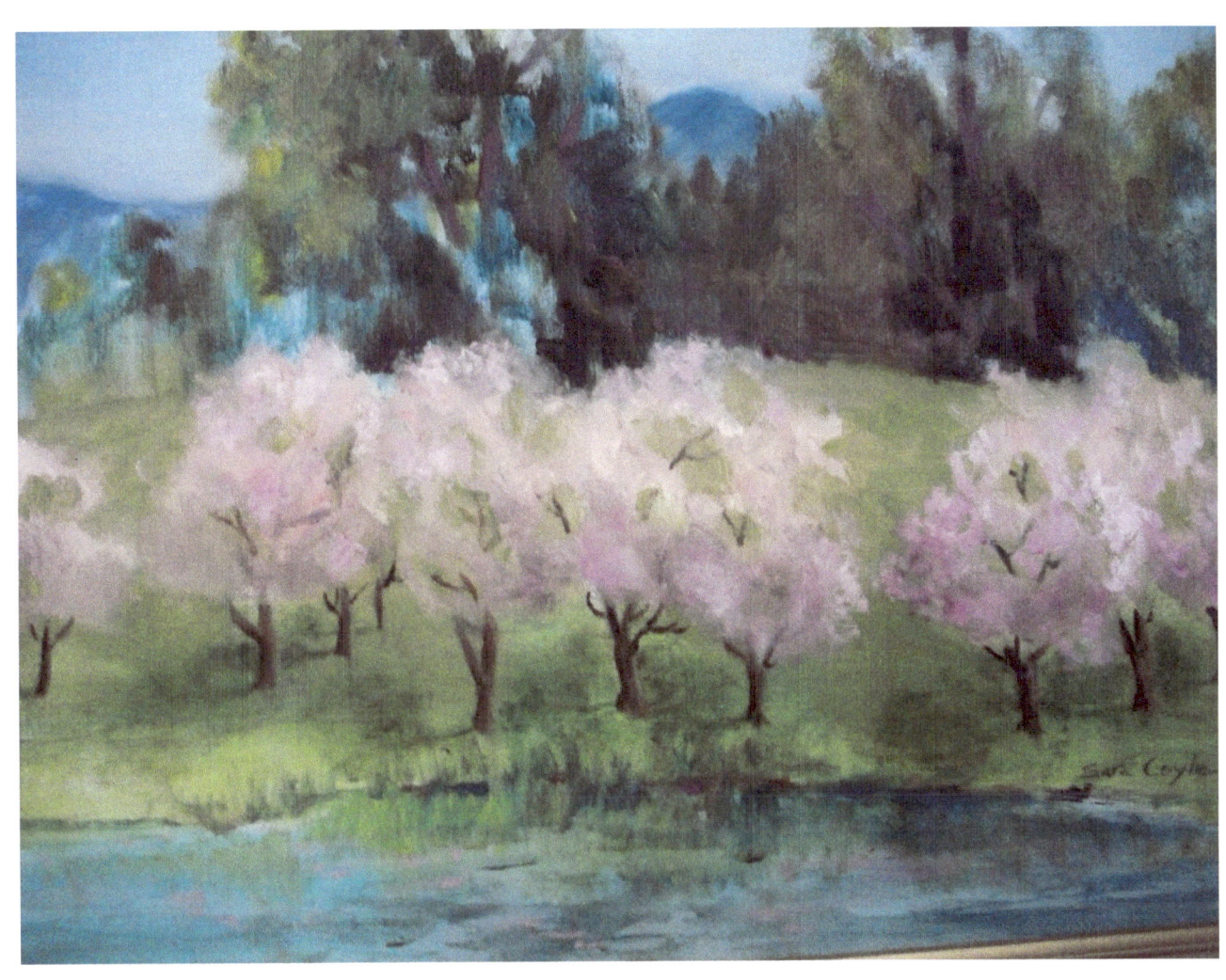

Lake Balboa, California

Cowboys

This old barn

waits for the

carriages and wagons

to come back

but silence reigns

while chickens

scratch the dirt

school children

watch the cowboys

do rope tricks

all deciding to be cowboys,

someday

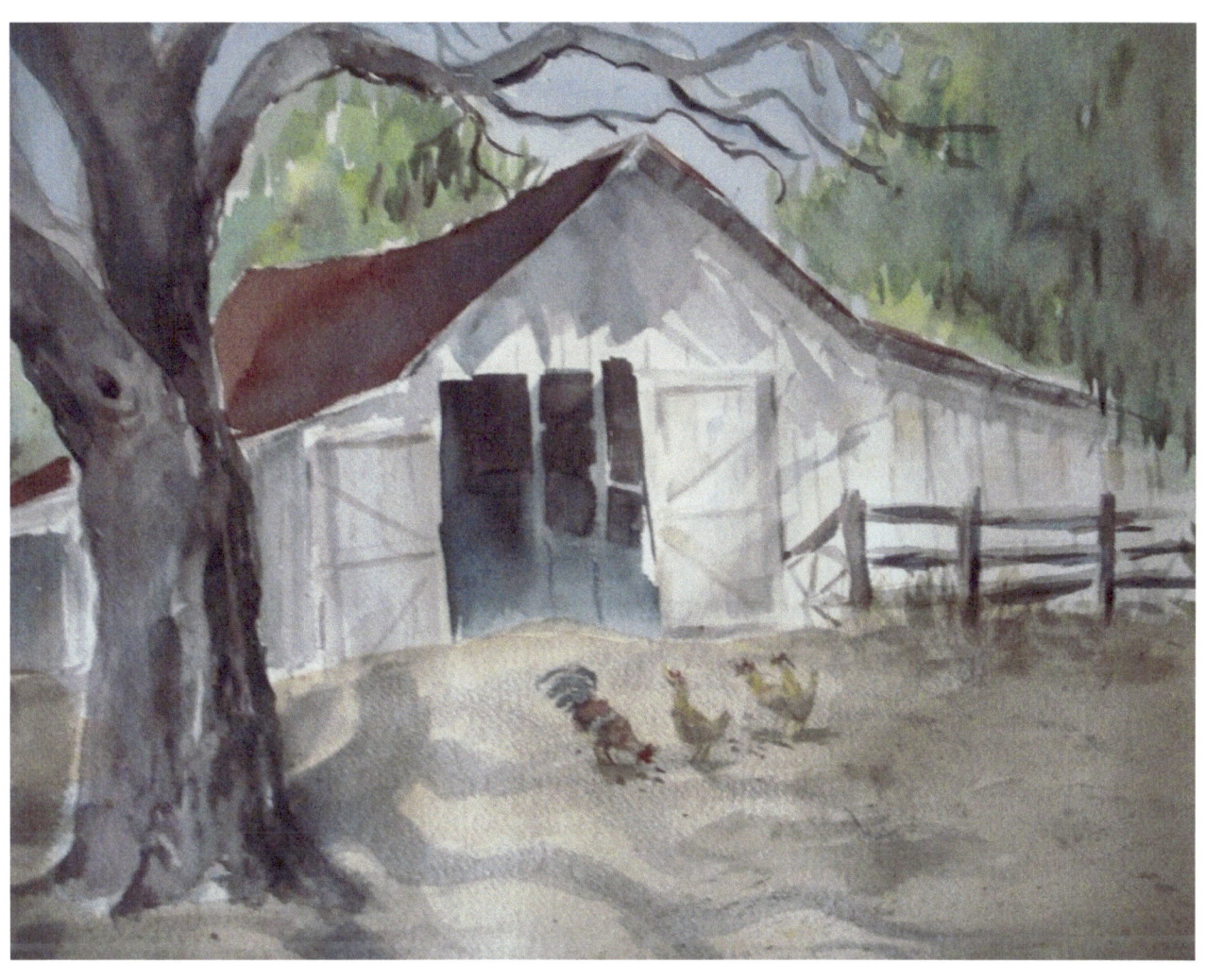

Leonis Adobe Barn Calabasas, California

Sunset on Rubio Street

The earth moves to night,

while the fiery sun

silently salutes us

with a crescendo

of shifting color.

The cymbals clash

and velvet surround us.

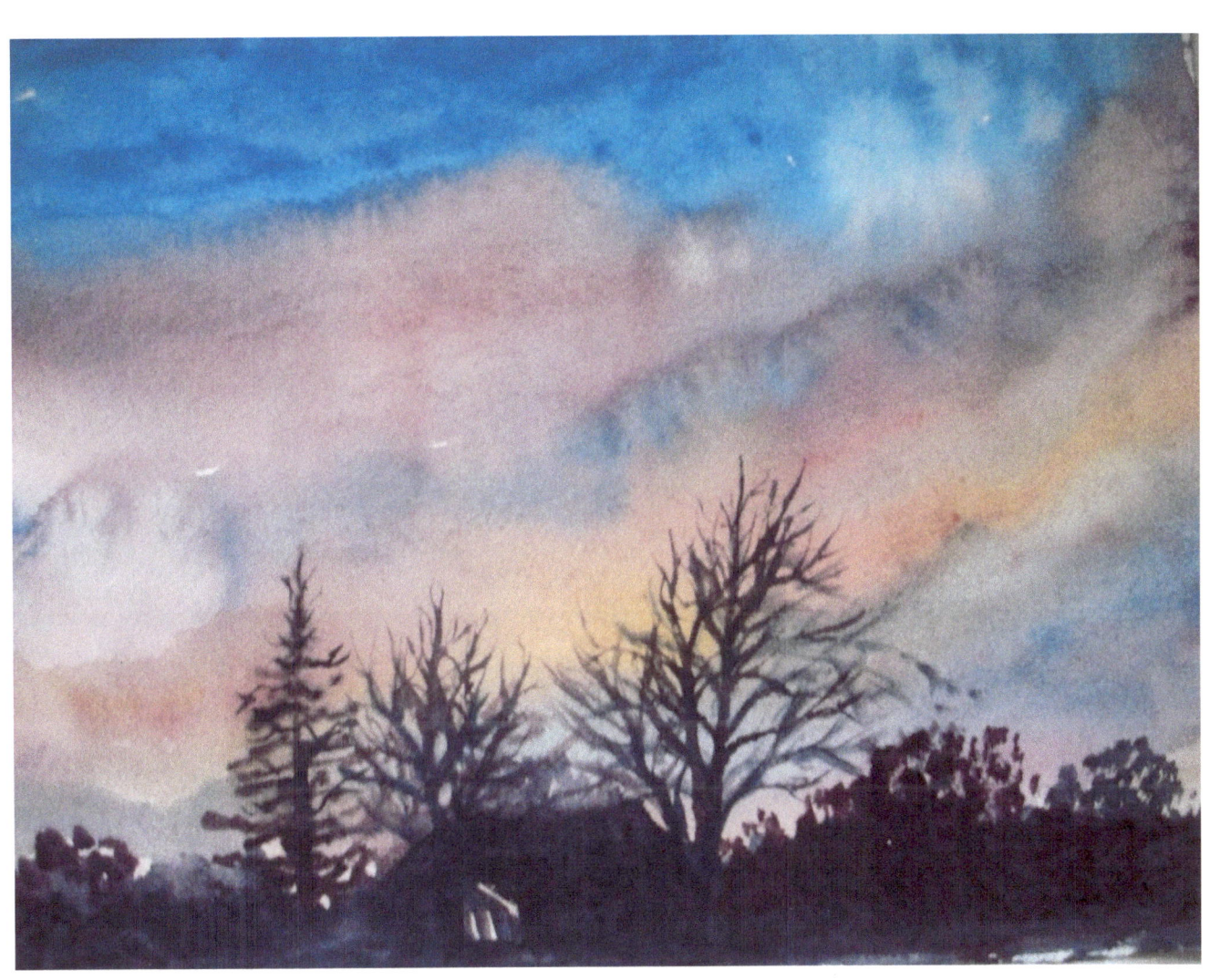

Eternal Beauty

The beauty of the world

Is revealed

In the rhythm

Of the waves.

The roaring waves

Roll to the shore,

Turn gentle, and

Tickle my feet.

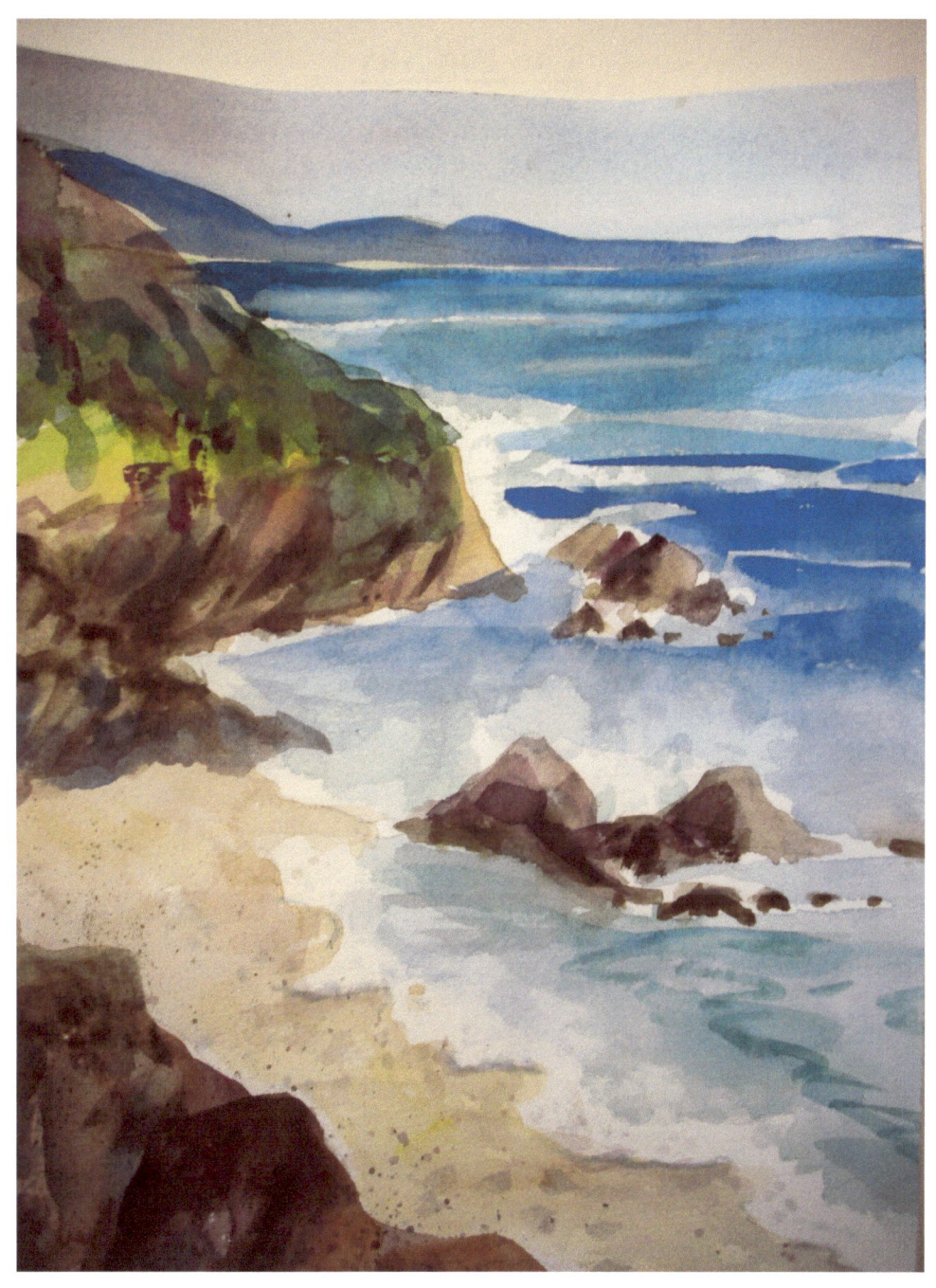

The Big Sky

Sitting in front

of the library

waiting,

watching the clouds

billowing

moving

changing color,

changing shape,

sheep on a hill

following their shepherd

glorious pictures

loving life's gifts.

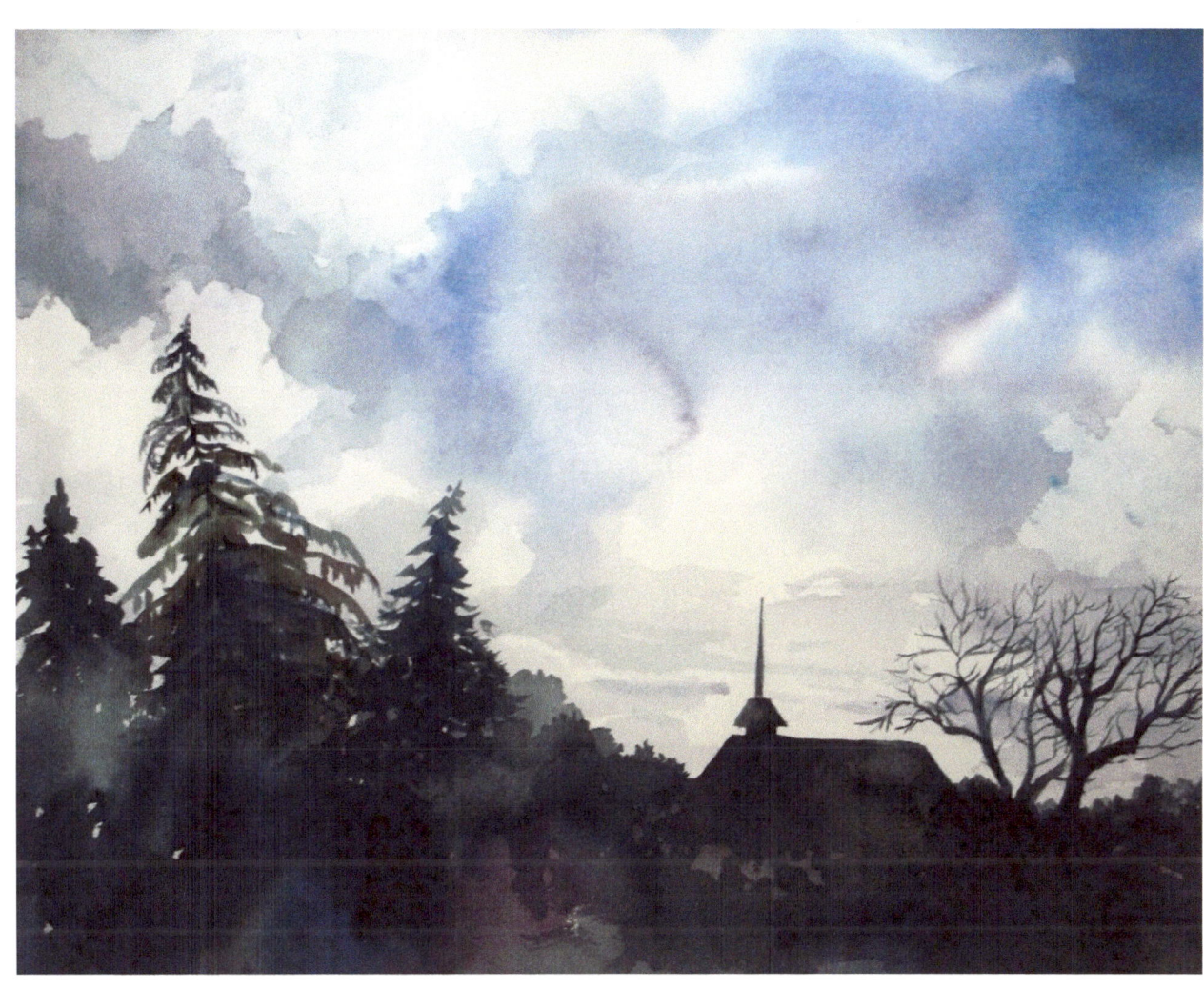

Descanso Paint Out

Mesmerized by
the tree reflections
bobbing in the water,
the flickering light on
the Japanese Maples,
and the soft music
of the flowing water,
I watch the Koi fish
swim together in the
spot of sunlight
filtering through the
gigantic oak trees.

The dropping seeds
make concentric circles
and hitting my head,
remind me that
my painting awaits me.

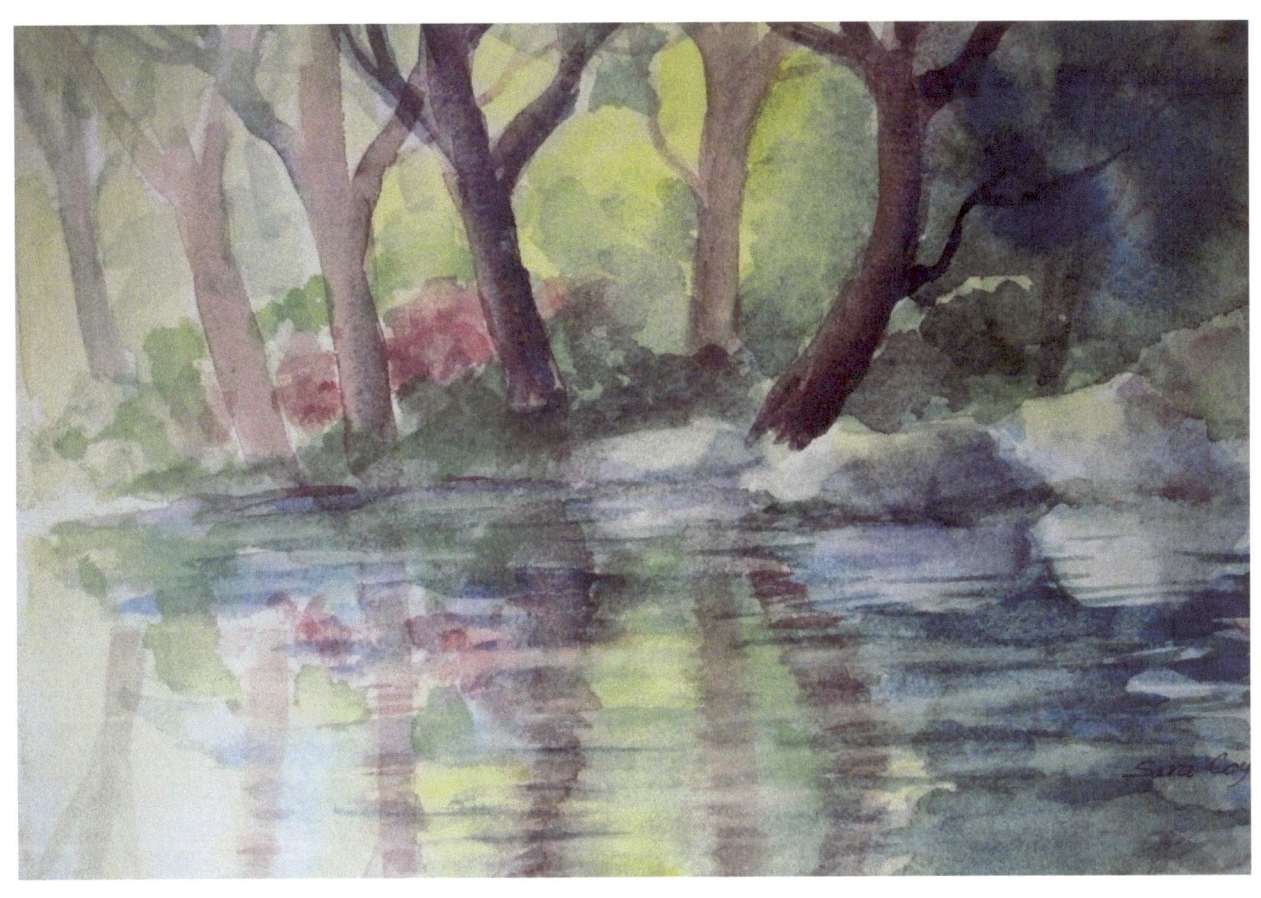

Descanso Gardens, La Canada, California

Farmland

California farms

Feed much of the United States

Most salads are grown here

The hills above this farm

Are emerald green after a rain

But because of our dry summer

They turn golden yellow

Farmers must dig

Deep wells and beg for water

To keep their crops growing.

Now the almond orchards

Eat up a lot of water

Since people are using almond milk so much

To put in their smoothie.

Farmers must be creative

Study the new trends

Work long hard hours

And pray for good crops.

So we will continue to have

Beautiful healthy produce.

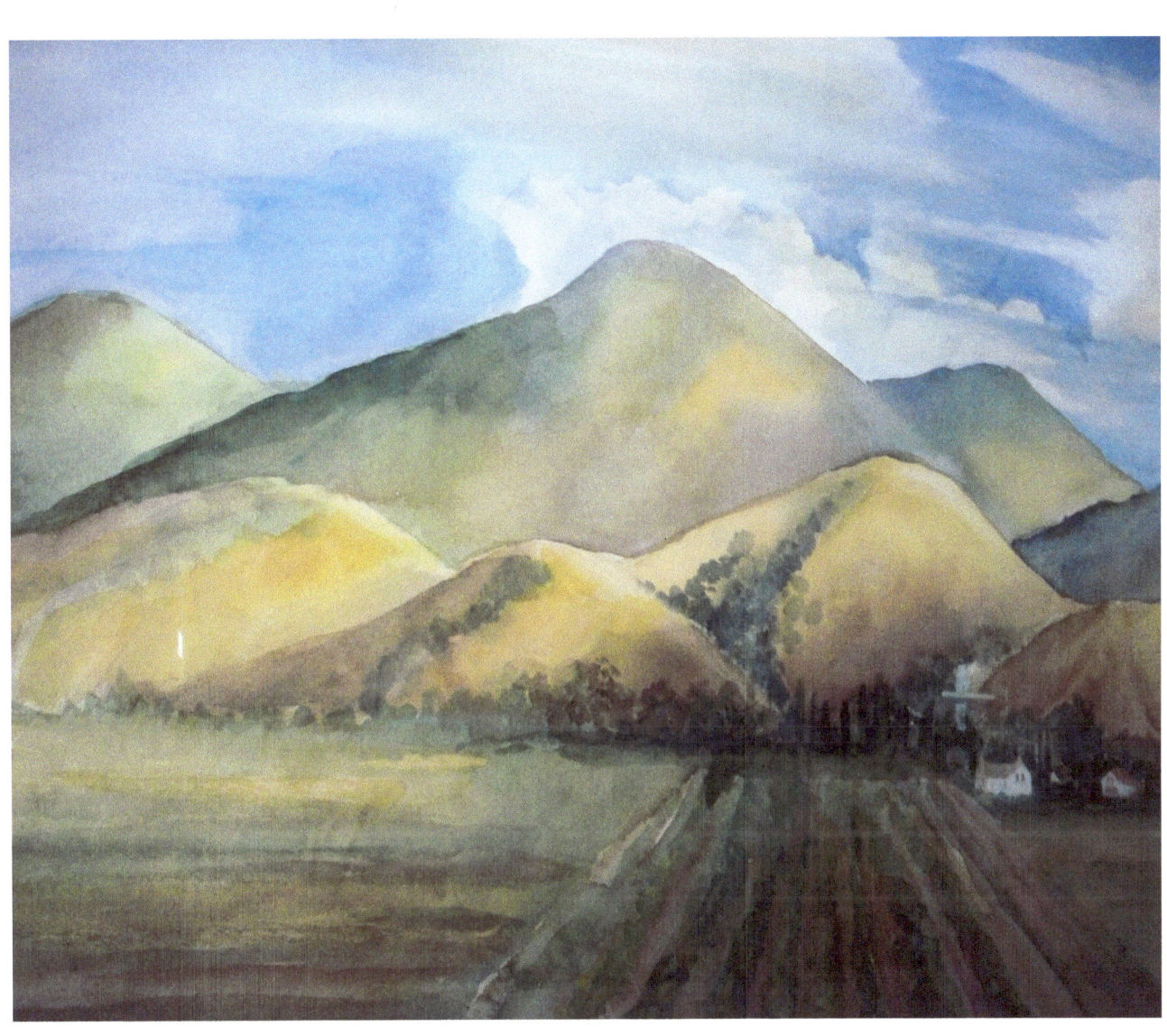

Ancient Wonder

Yosemite, a California jewel.

Majestic mountains

Against a cerulean sky.

Waterfalls splash rainbows

On ancient rocks below.

Autumn comes in

Bright golden colors,

Contrasting against the

Dark green of the pine and fir.

A sprinkling of powdered snow

Falls on this idyllic views.

A squirrel scampers across the road

Looking puzzled

As the snowflakes quickly disappear.

A peaceful scene of wonder.

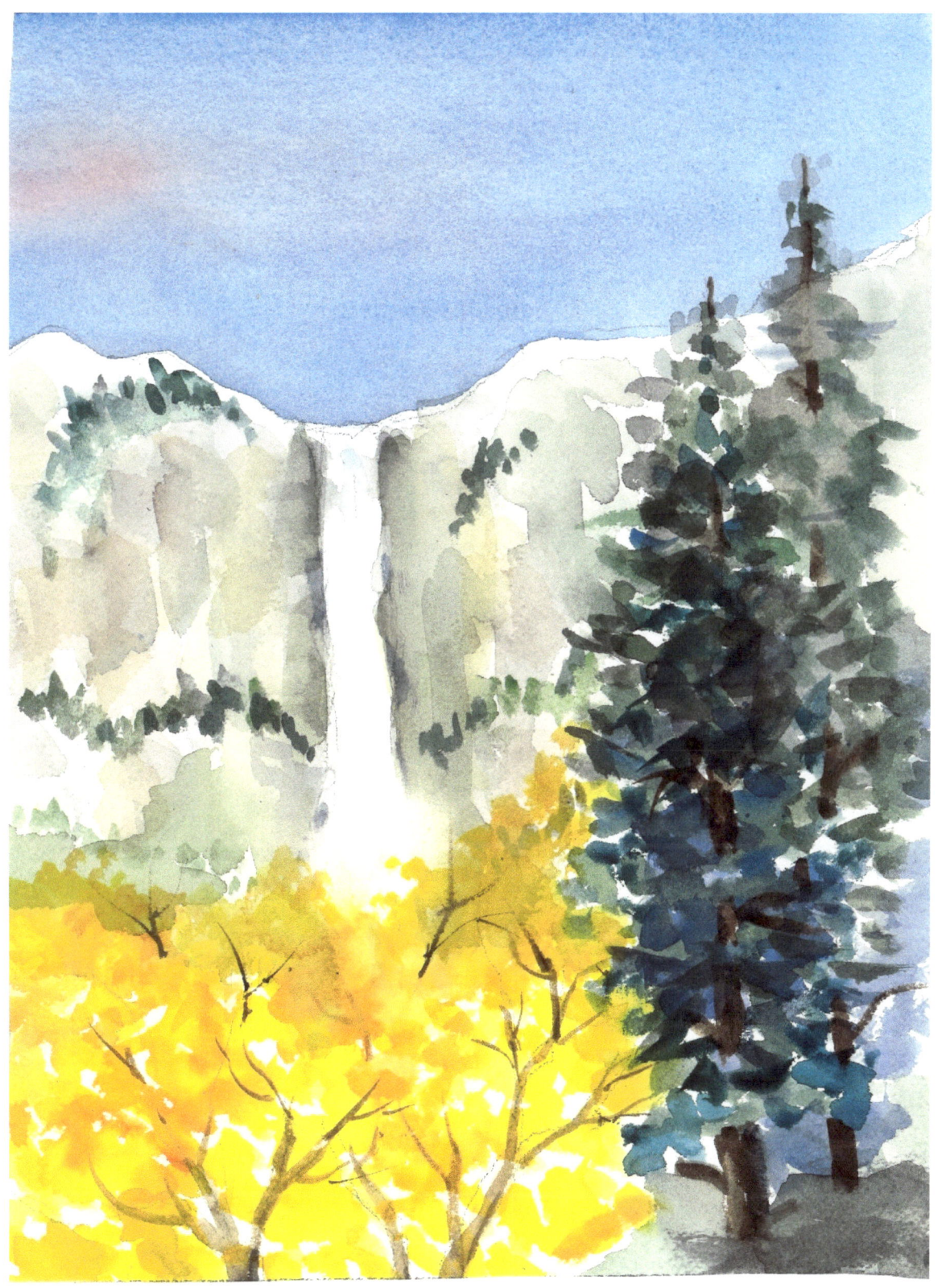

<u>Yosemite</u>

The air is crisp and clean
with smells of pine.
I hear the water
rushing down the stream
and the birds calling
to one another.
The trees reach
beyond the sky
and reflect in the water
deep beyond the earth.
The big boulders
are remnants of another age,
massive and rugged.
Time stands still for me,
as I stand in awe
of a place untouched by man.

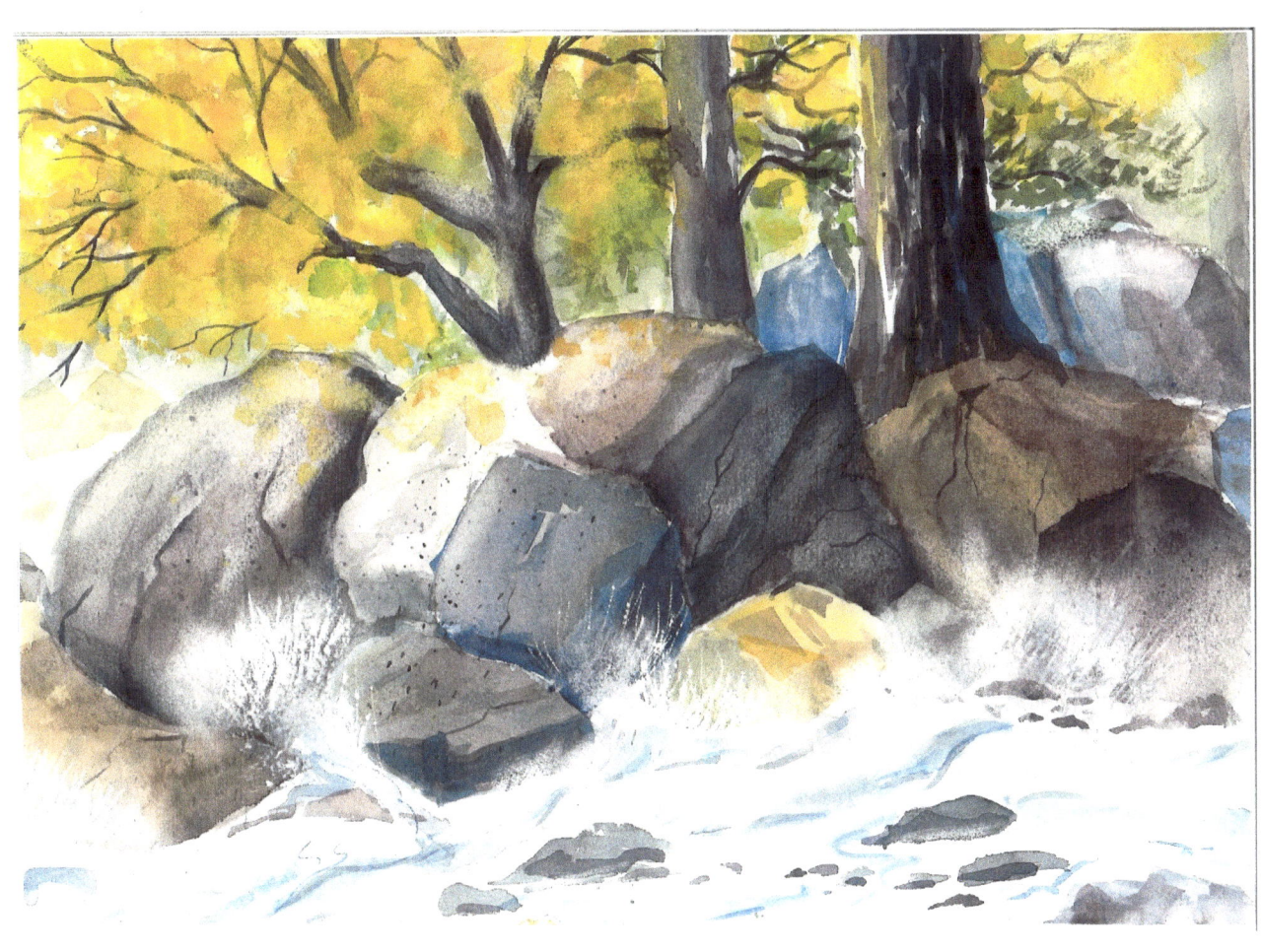

Nevada City

Nevada City reminds me

of New England in the fall.

Old houses, older trees,

autumn color falling to the ground,

filling up the sky.

These hilly streets,

piled high with golden coins

and red maple leaves.

Color, color everywhere,

houses playing hide and seek

among the trees.

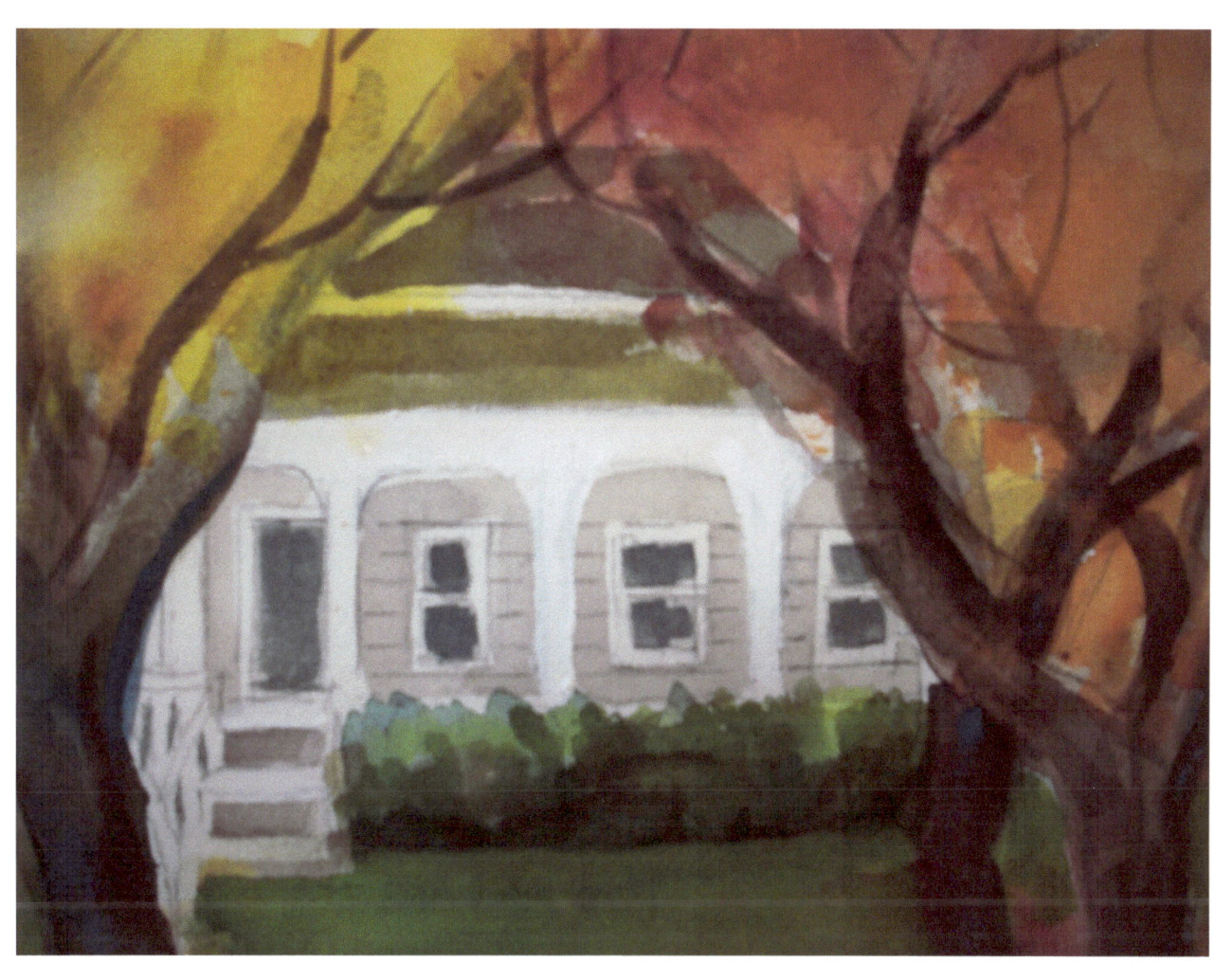

Plein Air Painting

Plein air painting

Near Lake Tahoe

The sparkling water

Reflecting gigantic trees

That quiets your mind

Sends chills down your spine

To be in the presence

Of amazing beauty.

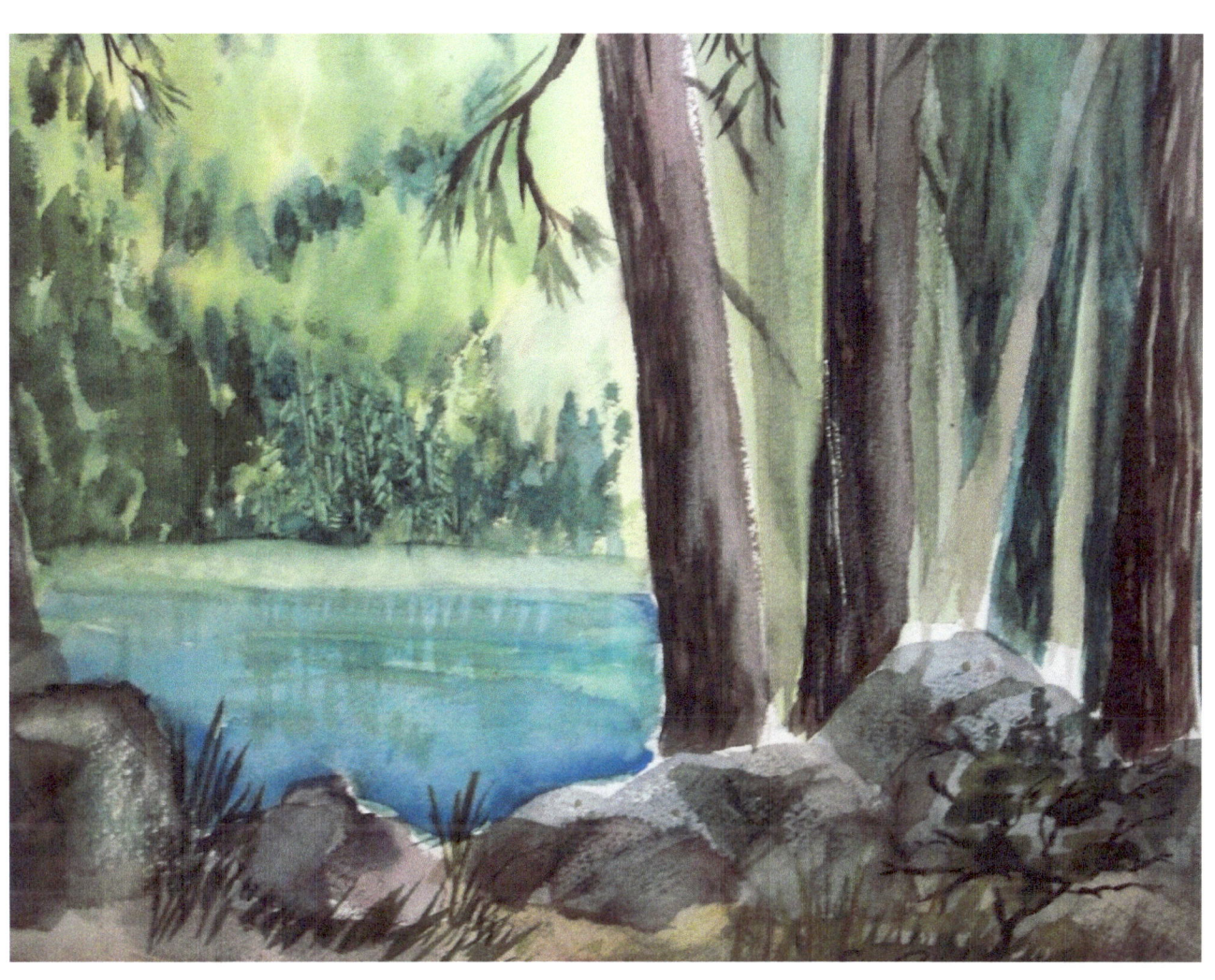

<u>Finding Peace in Monterey</u>

Walking along the beach

I find shade under

an ancient spreading tree.

The ocean is calm,

while the sea gulls

skim the water

looking for their meal.

I hear the waves splash,

smell the salty air,

and feel the sand

between my toes.

This peaceful scene

brings me joy.

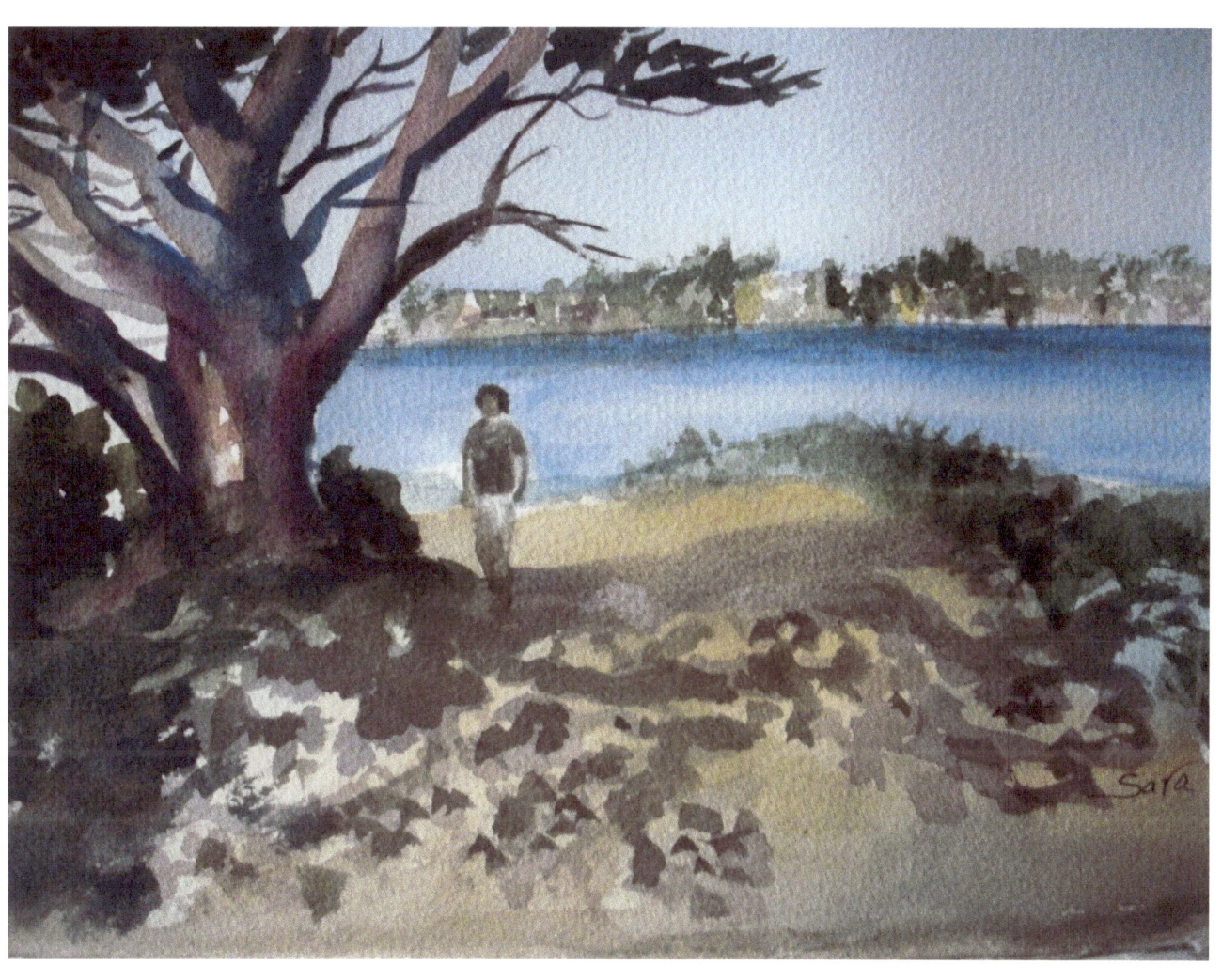

Ol' Mississippi

Stepping back in time
we lean against the railing
on our paddle wheel boat
rolling down the
Ole' Mississippi.
Now, reflections of the trees
near the river bank
move slowly by us.
Coming to a small town
people line up to wave.
Later, watching the sun setting
while the Calliope music
speaks to us of another time.

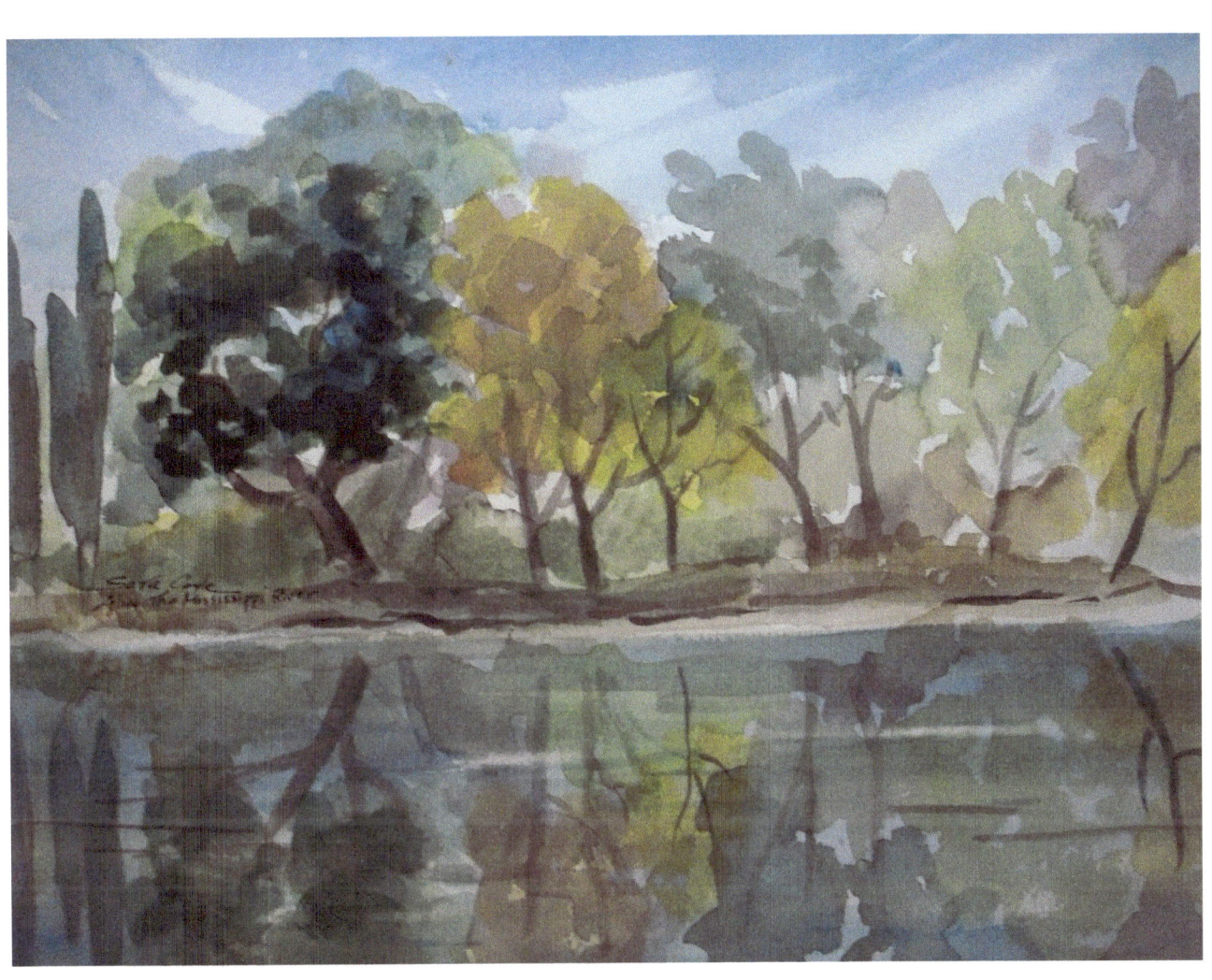

Broadway

Walking on Broadway,
with people rushing all day,
pushing carts and racks of clothes,
swinging shopping bags, briefcases,
or carrying a rose.
Signals say "Don't walk,"
but people still balk
at stopping on the curb.
Theaters with musicals superb,
line the street around Times Square.
You'll find tourists that stare
at gigantic animated billboards
and news that travels forward
in huge neon lights across the building.
Workers are busy welding
the newly renovated structures.
The mounted police are ready to obstruct
anyone who tries to commit a crime.
On the corner we see a mime
hoping someone will have a heart.
While on the side street a colorful cart
will sell rolls and coffee in a hurry
for all the New Yorkers who scurry.
The race is on, listen to the songs,
of New Yorkers that keep the beat,
even in the rain or Heat!

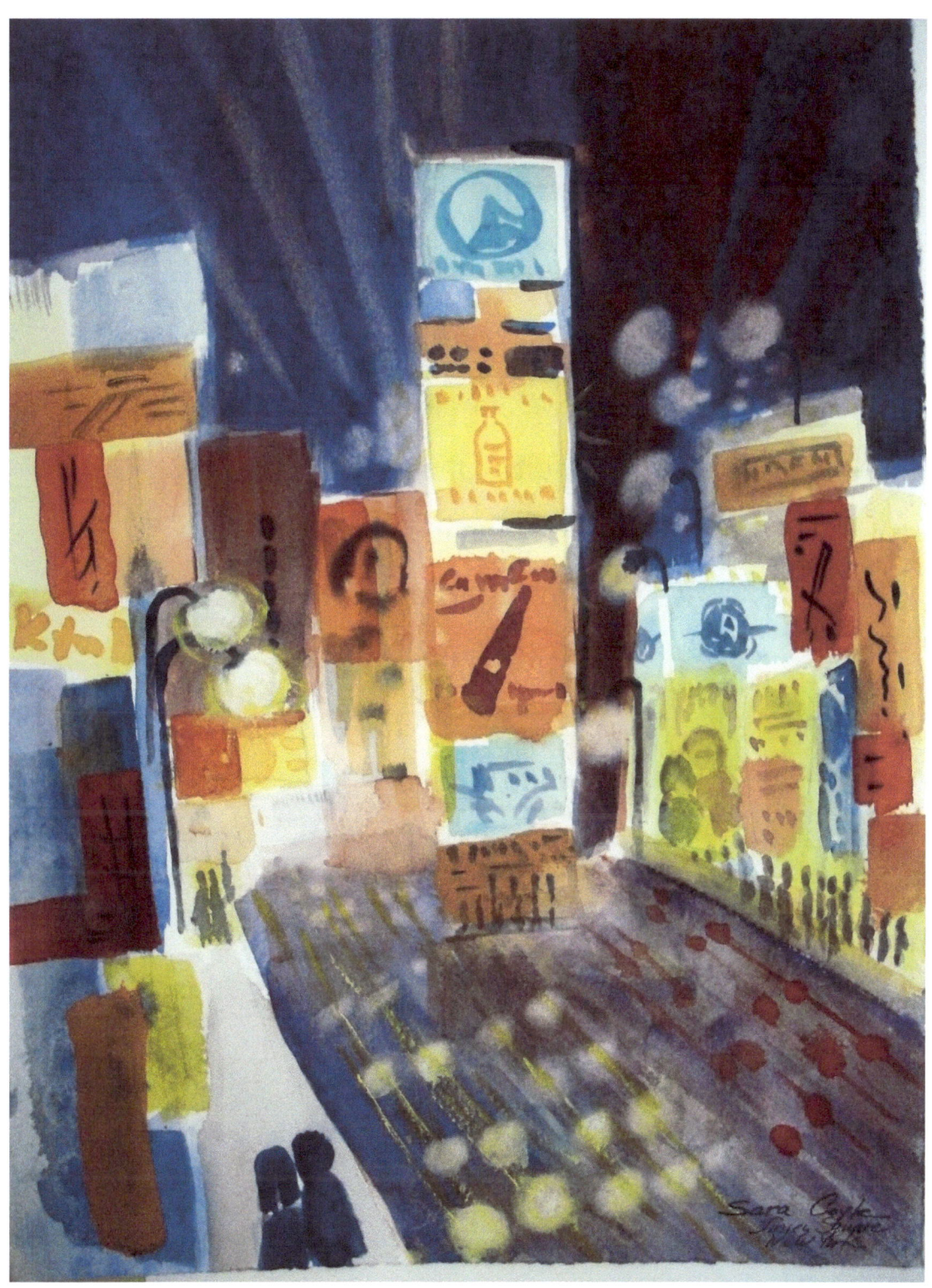

Niagara Falls

Dressed in yellow slickers
We all board our boat
Followed by the
Squawking sea gulls.
We move closer to the falls
And feel the spray
When we go under the falls.
All are wet
And surprised.
The thunderous roar
Surrounds us
Like the beat of
The earth's heart
Pouring out love.

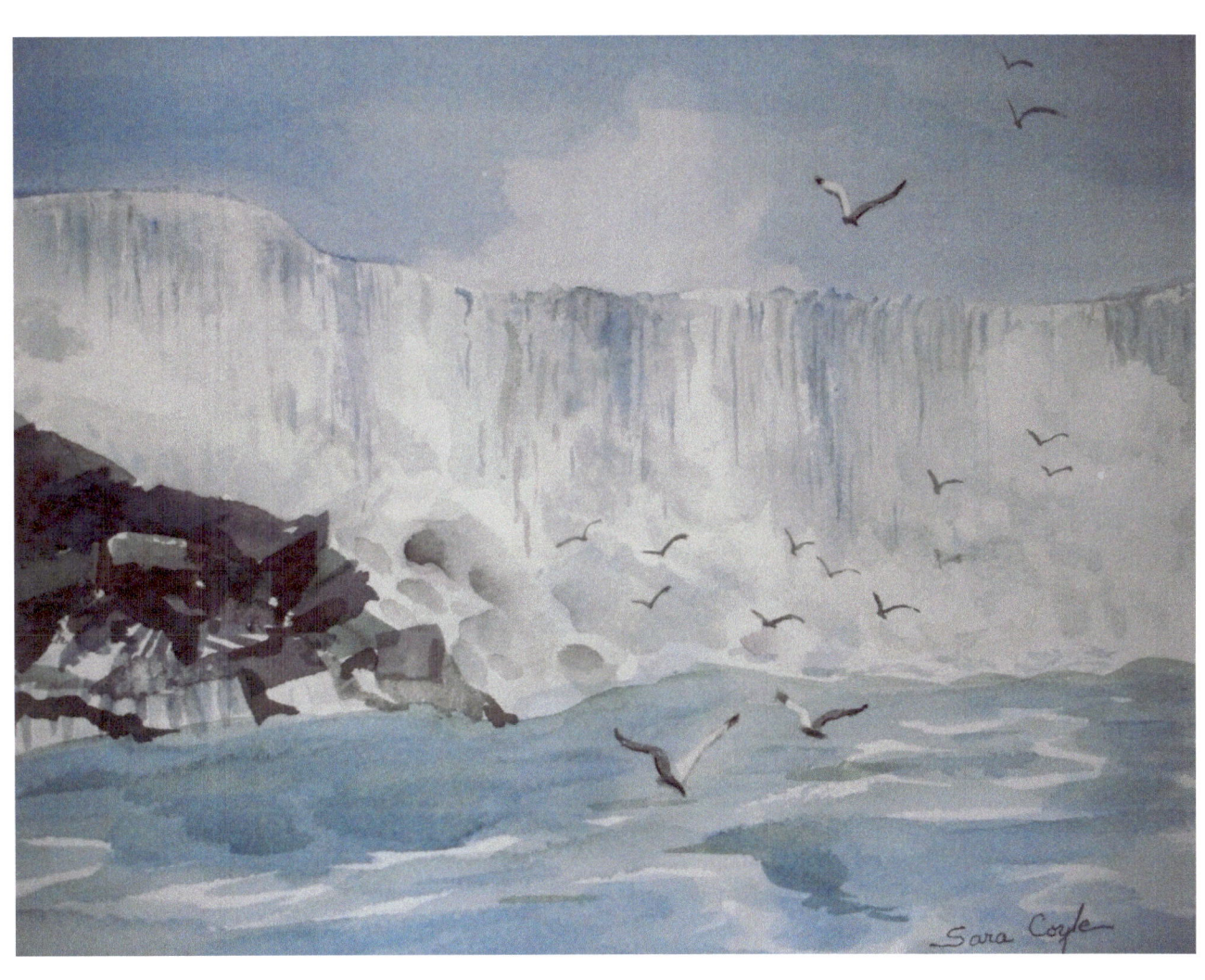

Surprise Guest

Our painting workshop was
on the 12th floor of the hotel
in Ventura, California.
Suddenly, a sea gull lands
outside our window.
He seems to be saying,
"I am your friendly sea gull,
waiting for a hand out.
I smell fish!
Come on guys, toss me one.
I'm waiting and watching,
but only see flashes of light.
I'm staring and begging,
but you only wave.
So, I'll just wave my wing,
as I fly off to the ocean,
where my dinner awaits."

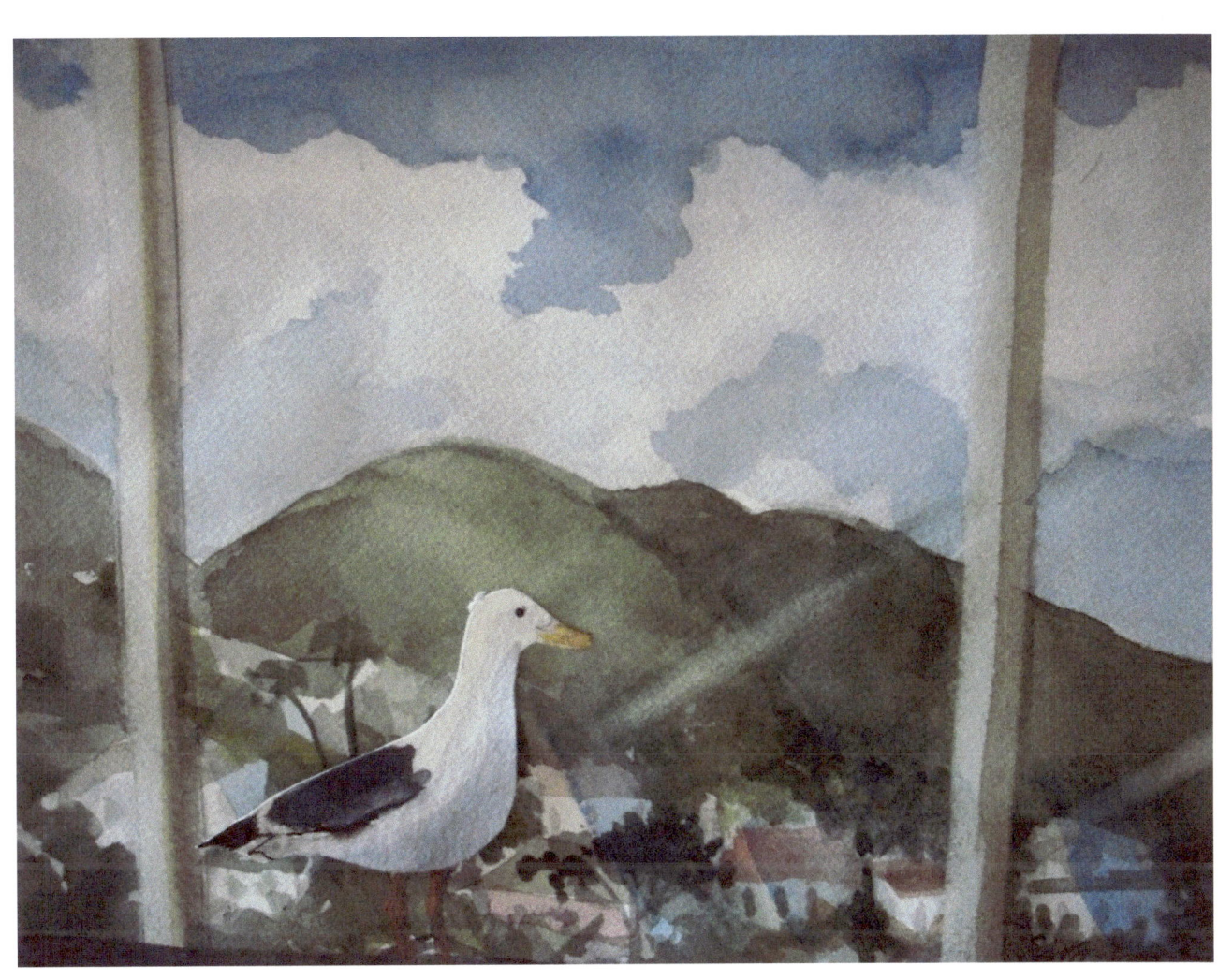

Colorado Mountains

Fresh air of Colorado mountains

stretch across a wide horizon

the train runs by

with its whistle blowing.

Bright yellow aspen contrast

against the mountain pine

with the red rocks

adding more color.

Put this scene

in your memory bank

to delight in it again.

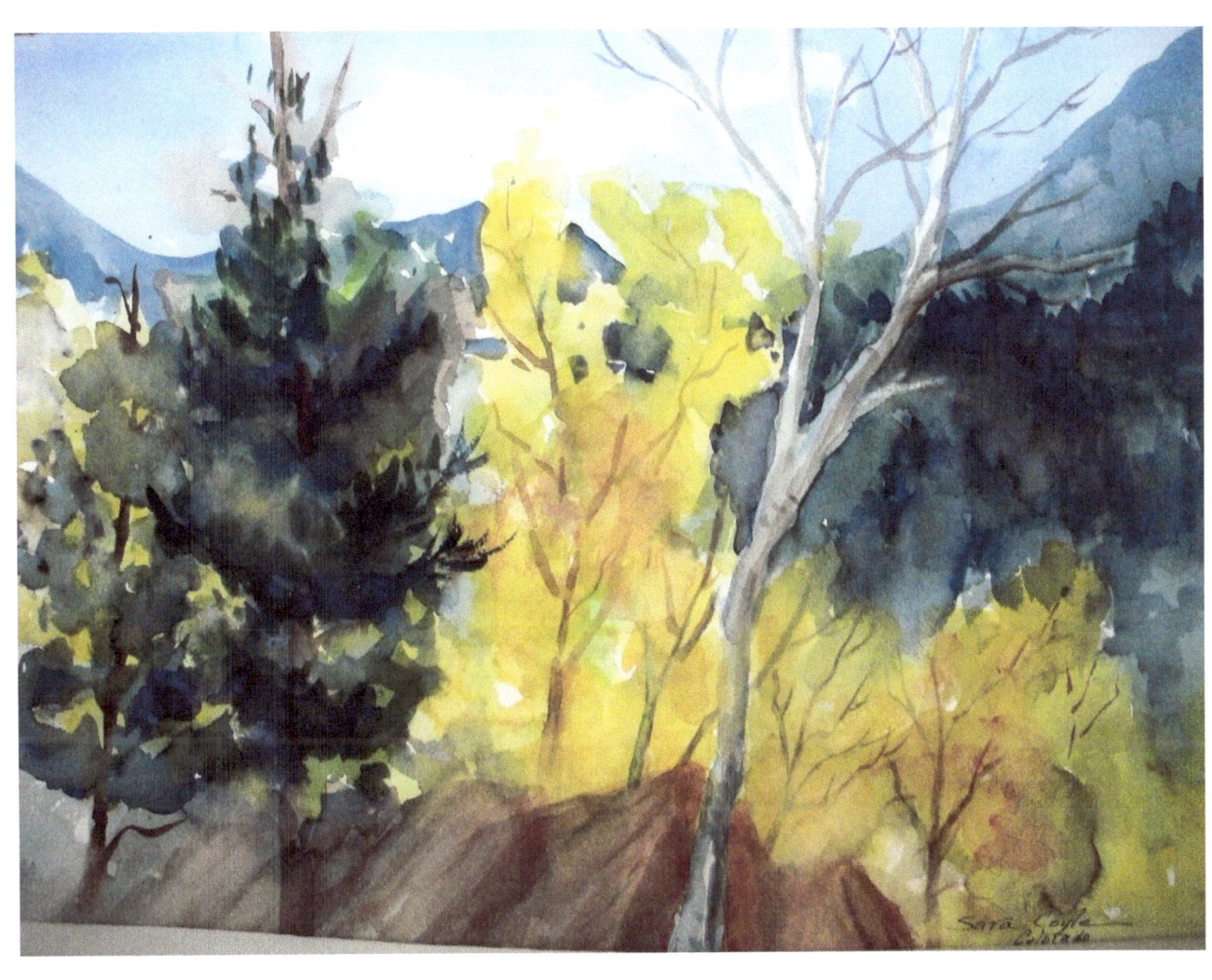

Alaska Sunrise

Cruising on the inland passage,
I wake up to a sunrise
of florescent colors that glow
and reflect the sea,
wrapping me in an amazing rapture.
Listening to the flapping waves
and feeling the crisp air on my cheek,
I float in a sea of wondrous color.
Good Morning, Alaska!

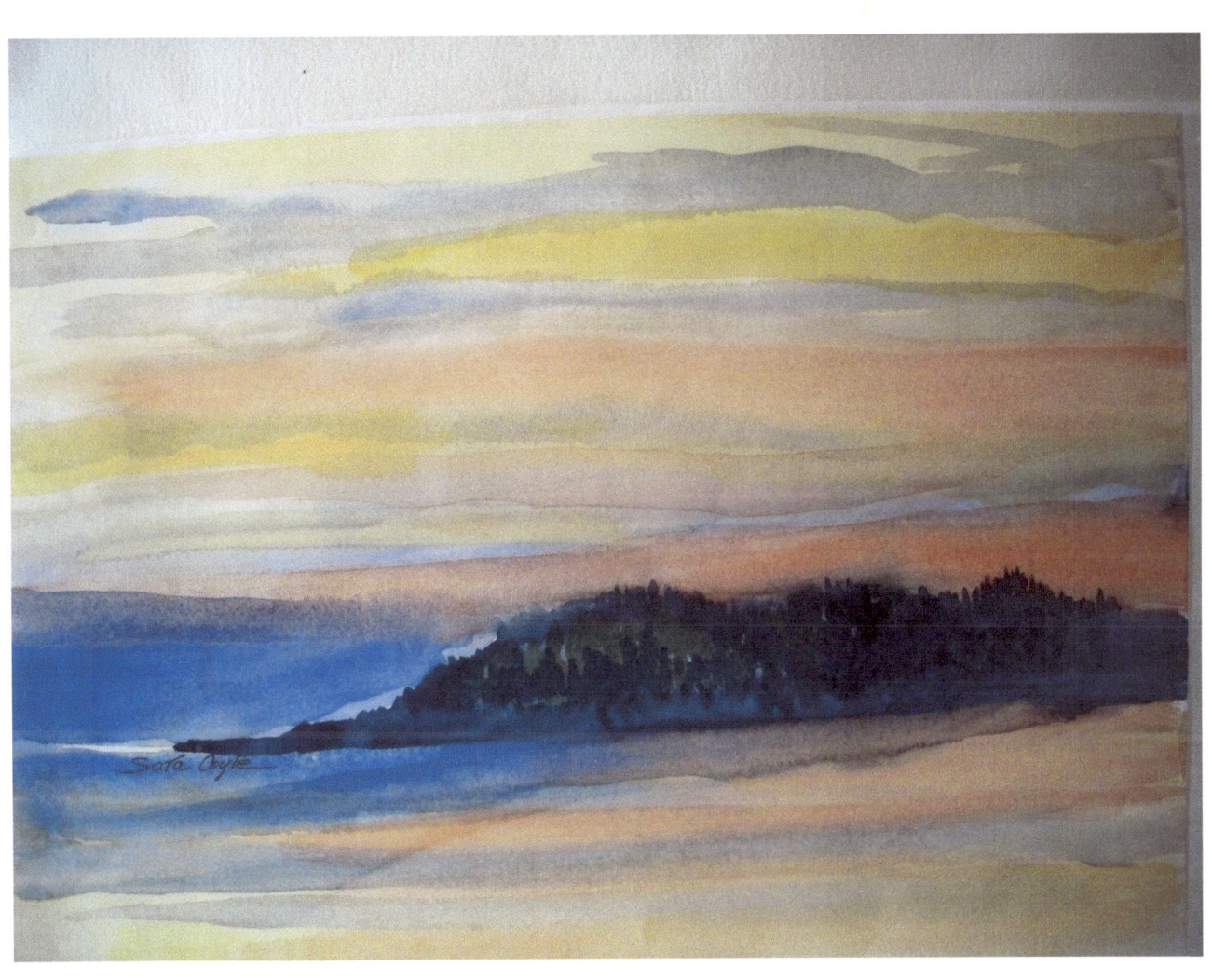

Glacier Bay

Through the window

of our cruise ship

we're watching big chunks

of the glacier crashing

down into the ocean

(called calving.)

This goes on continuously.

A sight to behold!

The sea gulls fly

close to all this commotion.

The passengers "ooh and Ahh!"

whenever they hear the crash

of nature's stage show!

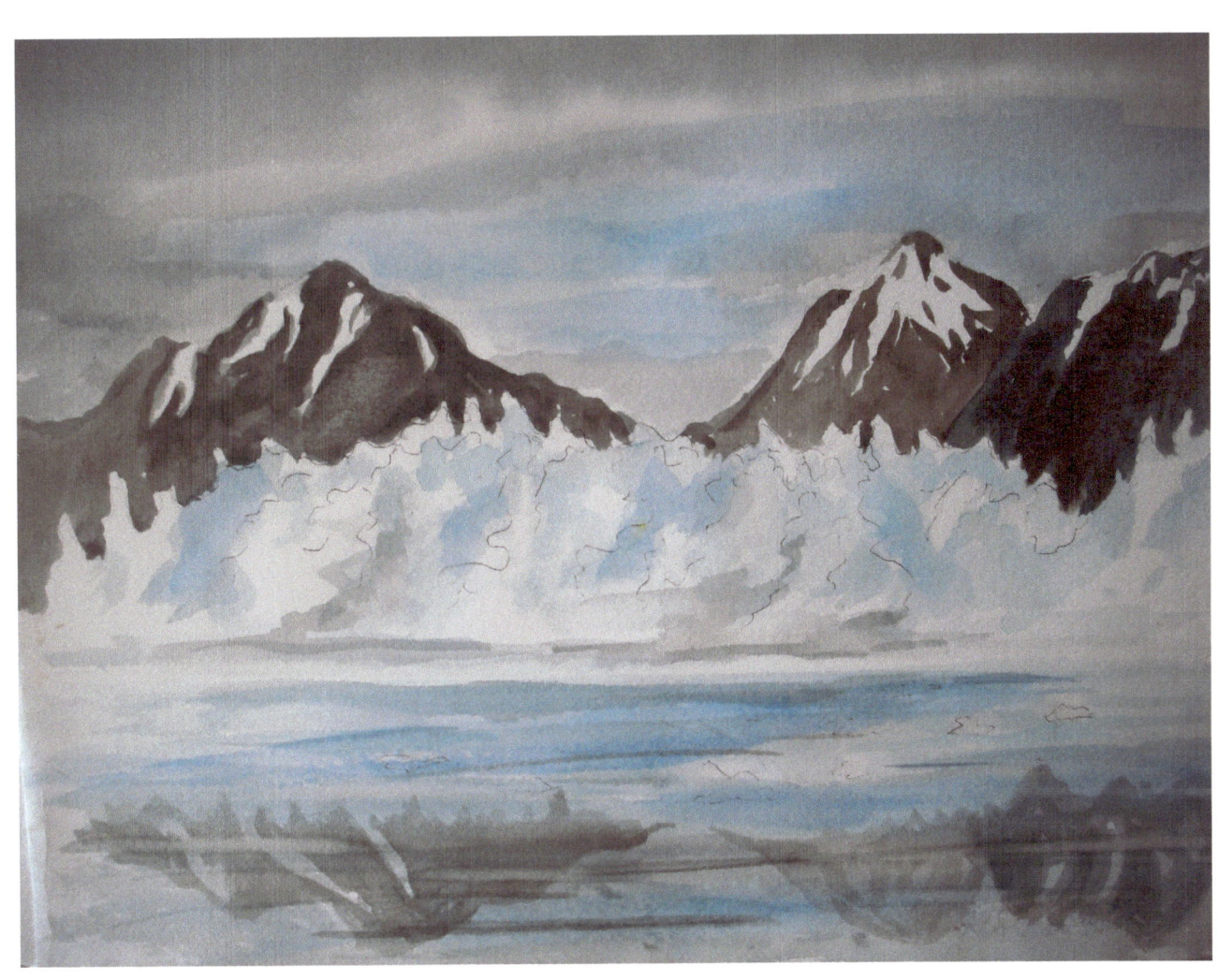

San Juan Islands

Hundreds of islands near Seattle

Stepping stones to Canada

Magnificent orca whales

Use this seawater

For their playground

Some islands are tiny towns

Others without any human inhabitants

And then islands with just a few rocks

My artist friend bought an island

Built a house

To be alone and paint

In this vast paradise.

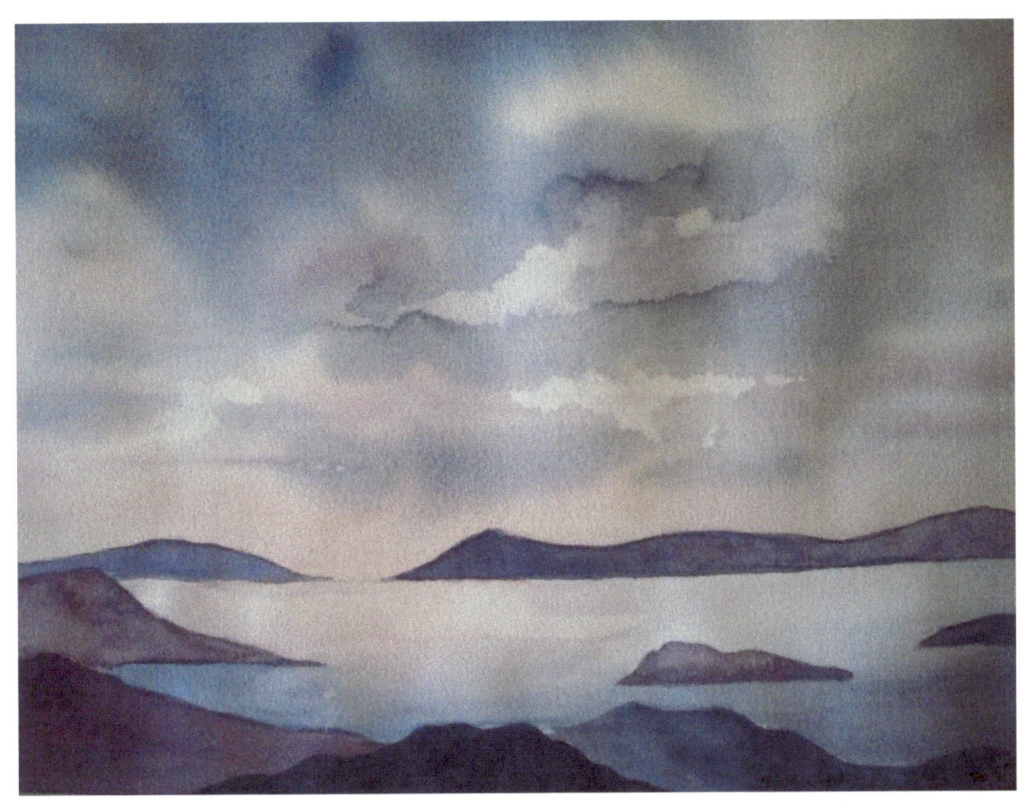

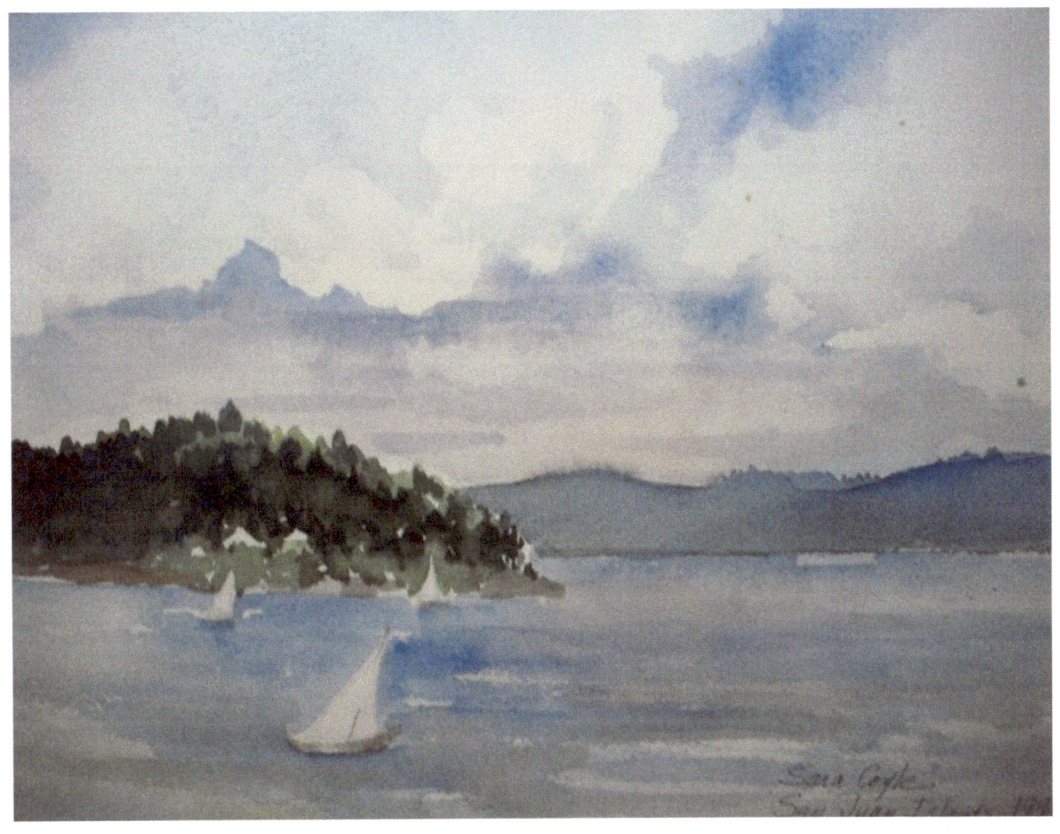

Silver Falls State Park, Oregon

The stately Douglas firs

Fill my lungs with the scent of the forest.

The beauty of the trees

Fill my soul with a forest symphony

At the base of these trees,

A waterfall plunges 178 feet

Over the cliff.

The silver water sparkles,

As it roars by me,

Sending chills down my spine,

While misting my face.

A waterfall of such power!

Forever falling, forever a wonder!

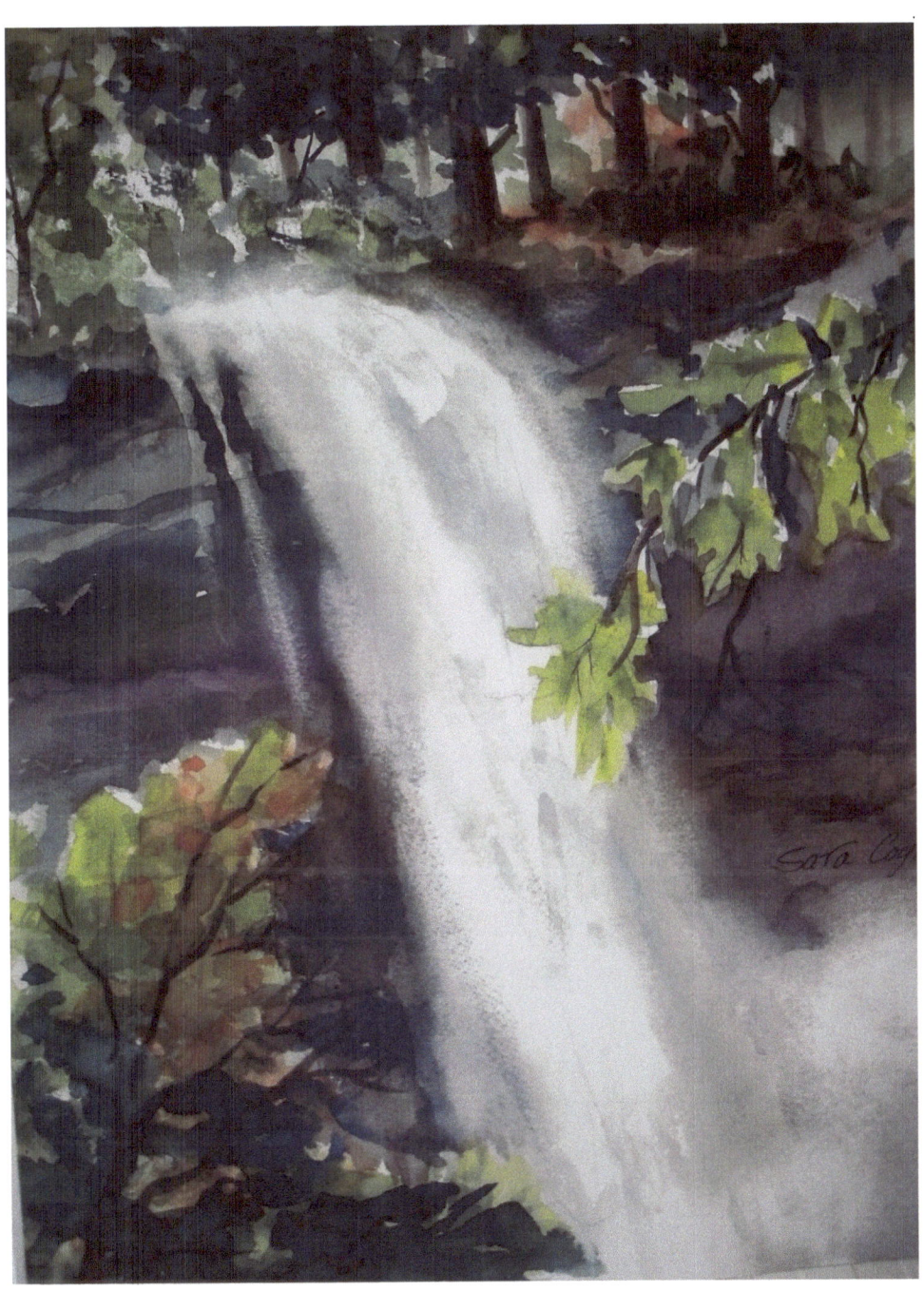

A Simple Life

The Amish can teach us
Many ideas about living
Living the simple life
Farming to feed your family
Cooking healthy food
Sewing your clothes
Helping your neighbor
When he's building his barn
And needs an extra hand.
We all need to help
Our neighbors
Like the Amish
Are taught to do.
A simple life is what we all need
In this fast paced world.

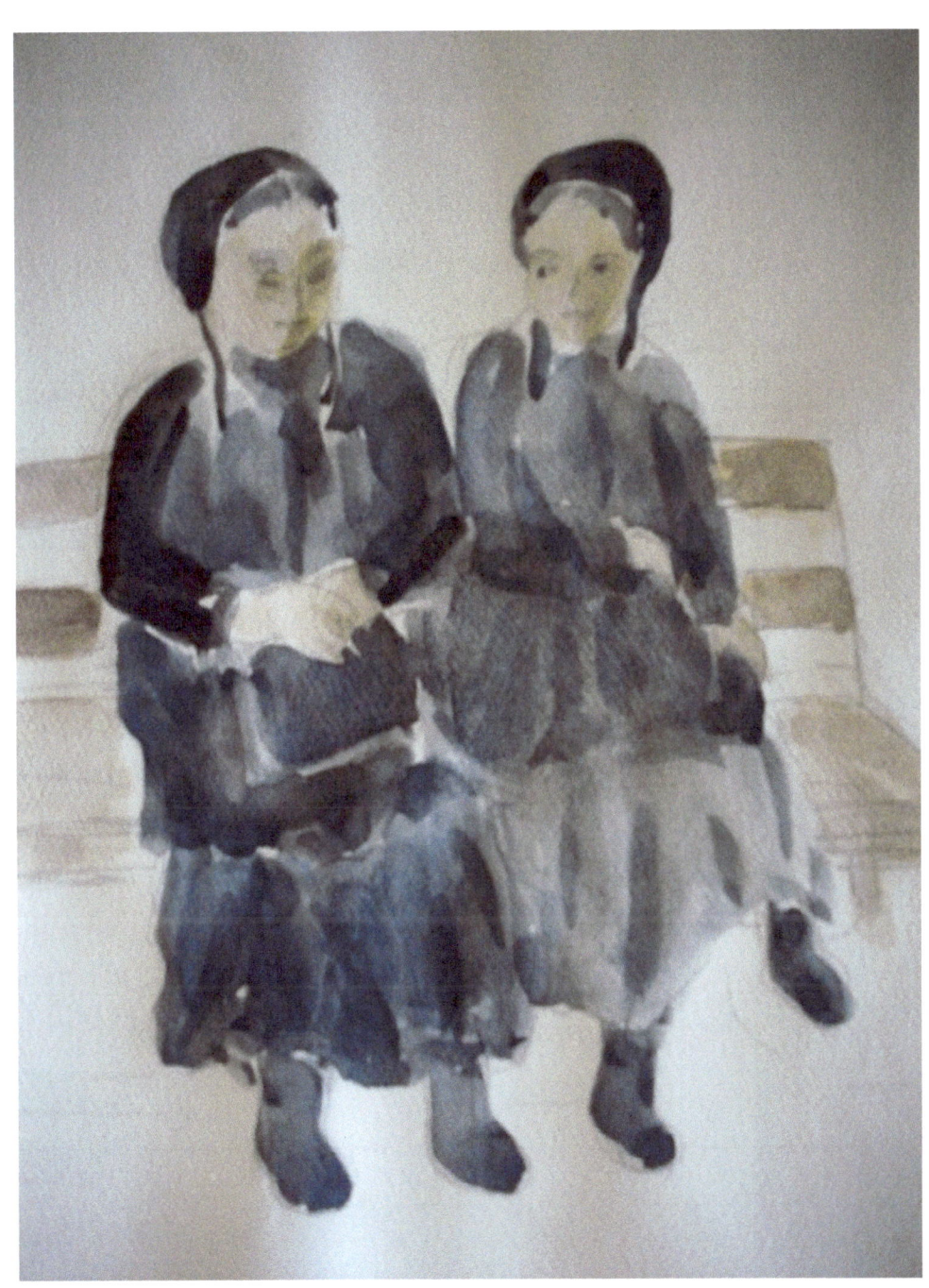

Utah

Our Road Scholars

Met in Saint George

To travel to the

Extraordinary formations

In Bryce and Zion Canyons,

All sculpted during

Millions of years,

From glaciers, water, and wind.

All this beauty

Has taken time.

As we look out

At this haunting sight,

Time stands still for us.

The artist's giant sculptures bring us bliss.

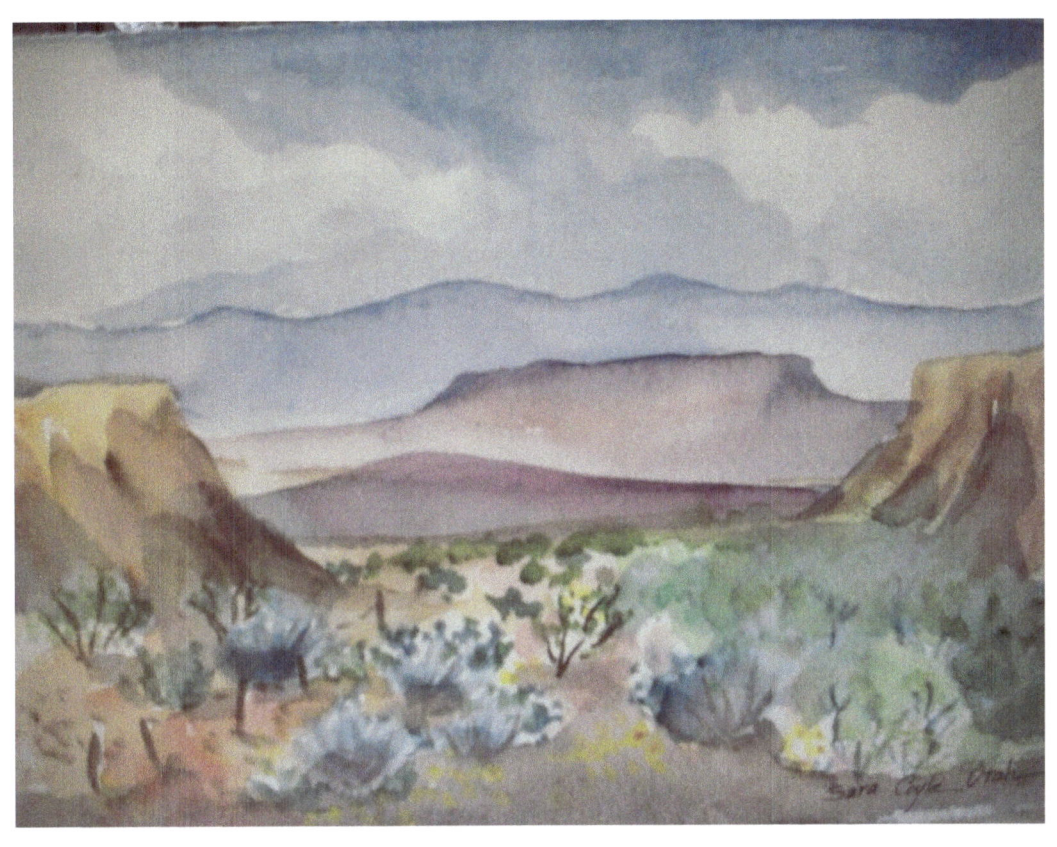

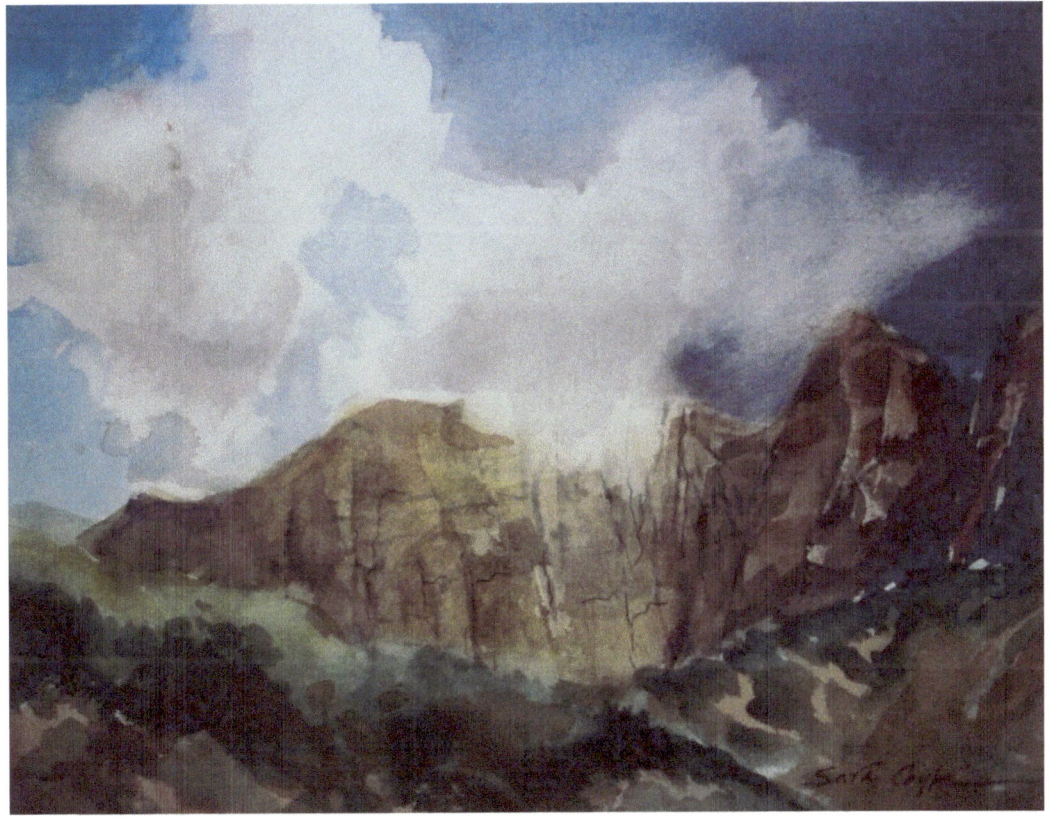

Hawaii

Lush green mountains

Waterfalls and volcanos

Scrumptious luaus

Hula dancers

Sway in rhythm

To Hawaiian music

While palm trees sway in the breeze

Muscular climbers

Spring up the coconut palm

To fetch a coconut

To drink and eat

Sunsets the color

Of Hawaiian rainbows

Aloha to all!

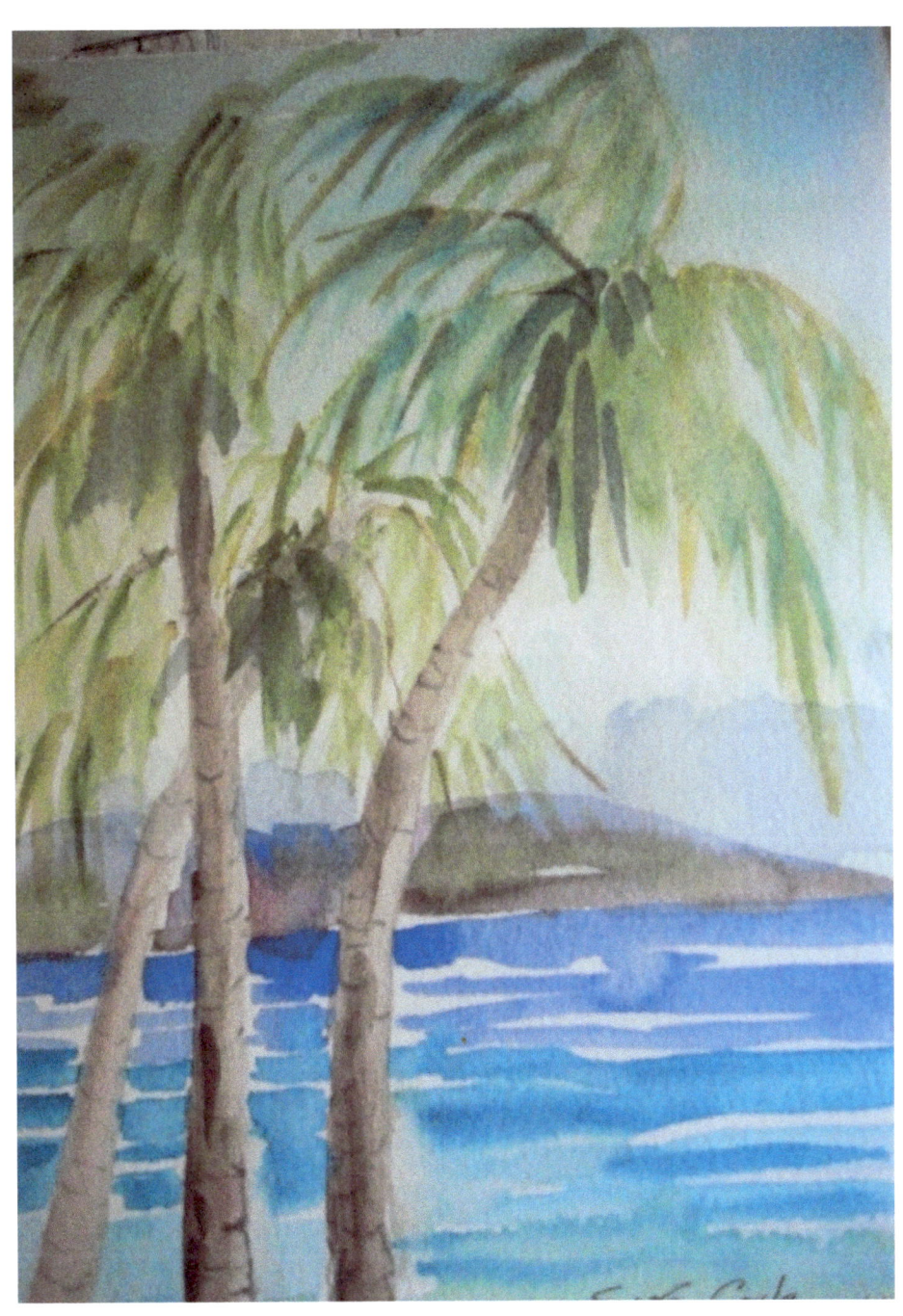

England

Flying low over

A patchwork quilt of farmland

Edged by hedgerows and low rock walls,

We land in London.

We travel the narrow winding roads

Passing small towns with flowers everywhere.

The cottages with chimneys on both ends

Grow flowers out of every window.

Appearing out of the mist

The ancient stone castles

Are mysterious and often deserted.

History is everywhere.

These delightful, friendly people

Have accents that are music to our ears.

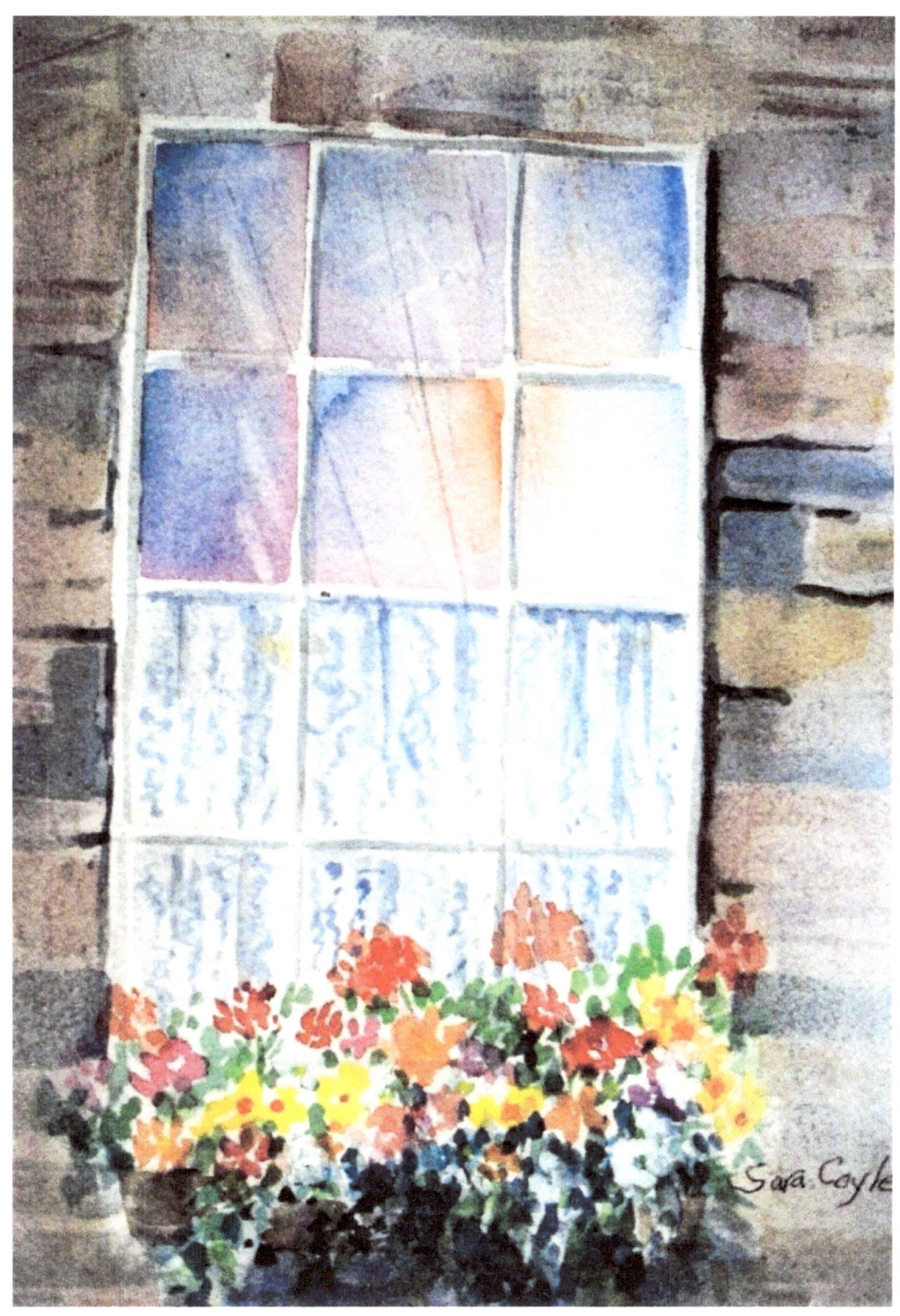

Home of Heather

Sweet blooms of heather
Climb over the rocks
Greeting those who pass by.

On the other side of the road
The green fields hide the Leprechaun,
While the cars wait
For the sheep to cross the road.
The shepherd hustles them
On with his dog following.

The slow pace of life here
Makes you happy to be
In Ireland.
The Irish comedians
Make everyone laugh
Even during difficult times.
Erin go Braugh!

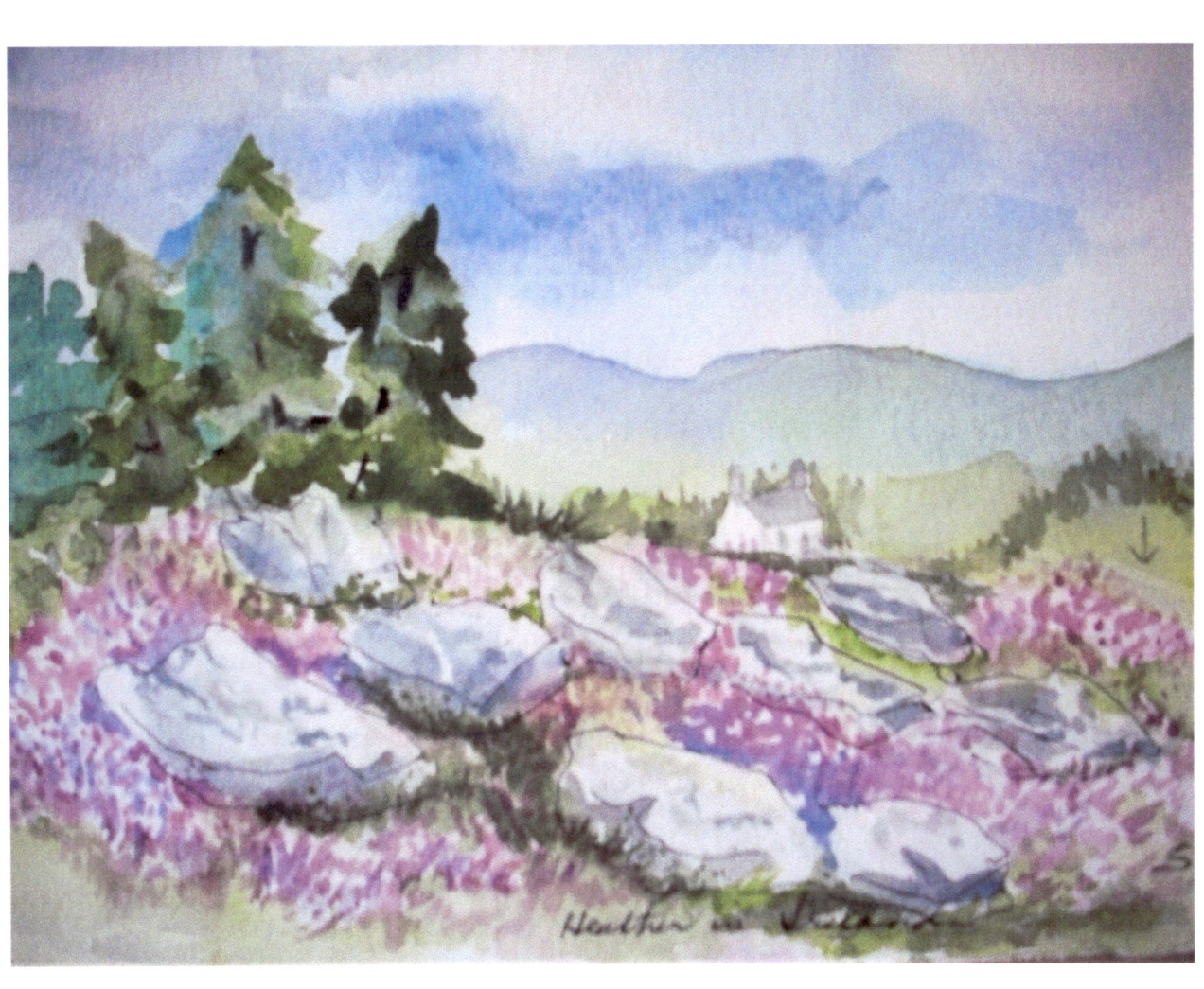

Scotland

Traveling the rolling hills
Of the countryside of Scotland
We reach Edinburgh
Where we have dinner.

On the bridge in Edinburgh,
We sang Amazing Grace,
Accompanied by our tour guide, Philip,
Dressed in kilts,
Playing the bagpipes.
One man in our group
Took off his hat,
As if asking for a handout.
And the local drunk looked astonished.
Laughter is good for the soul.
Beauty is good for the spirit.
Traveling opens your eyes to the world.

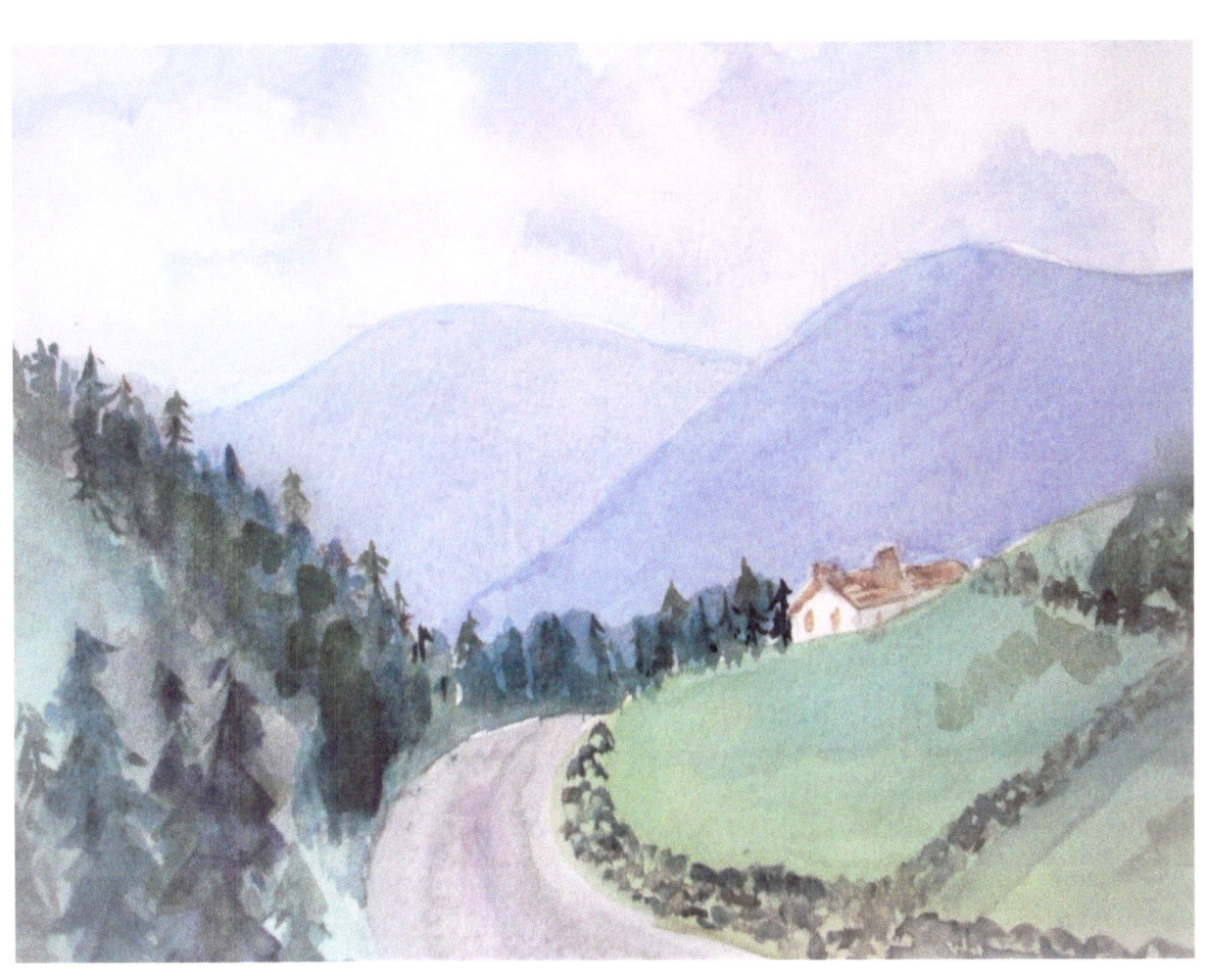

Paris

A sunny day, windows open wide
Sidewalk cafes, busy
Parisians huddled together
Eating off frisbee size tables
Soaking up sunshine
Piping hot baguettes
Carried under arm
While pulling off pieces
Peddling a bicycle.
Sidewalk kisses on each cheek
Older men wearing berets
Young ones wearing helmets.
Zipping around on motor scooters
Look out! When you cross the street.

Bonjour, merci beaucoup, sil vous plait
Words that sing while Paris
Wakes from winter.
A tout a l'heure!

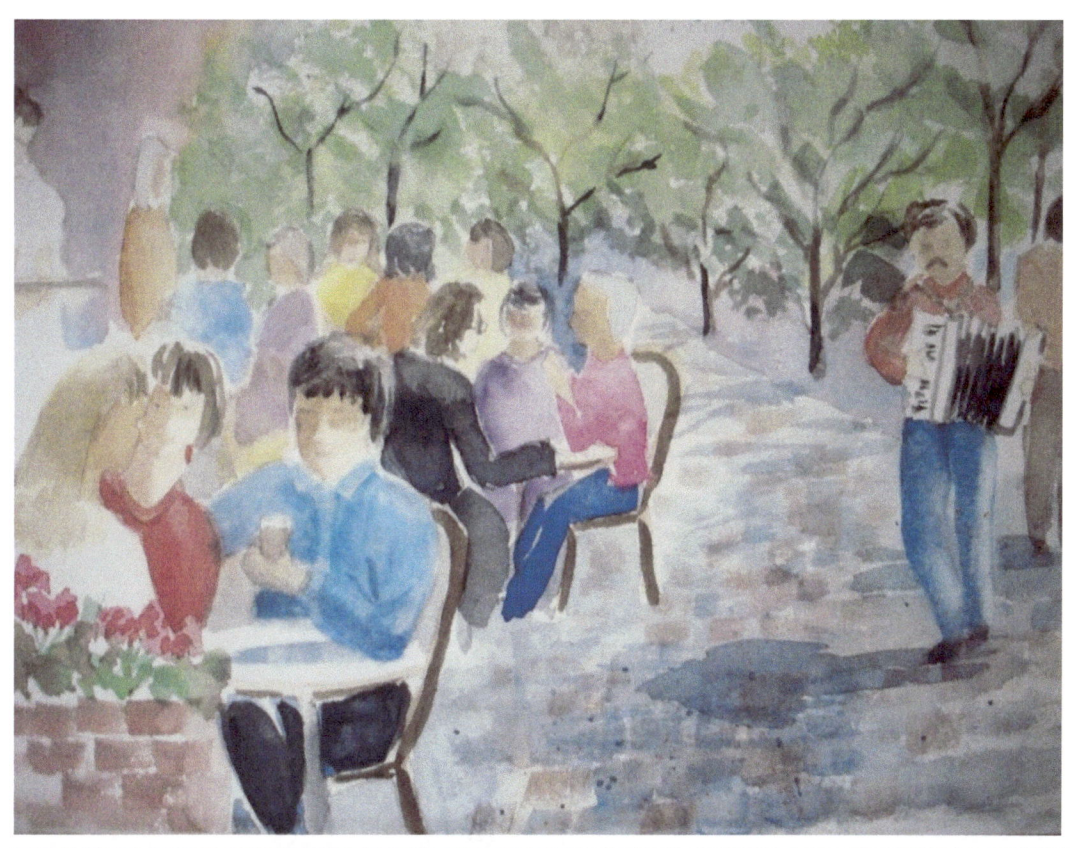
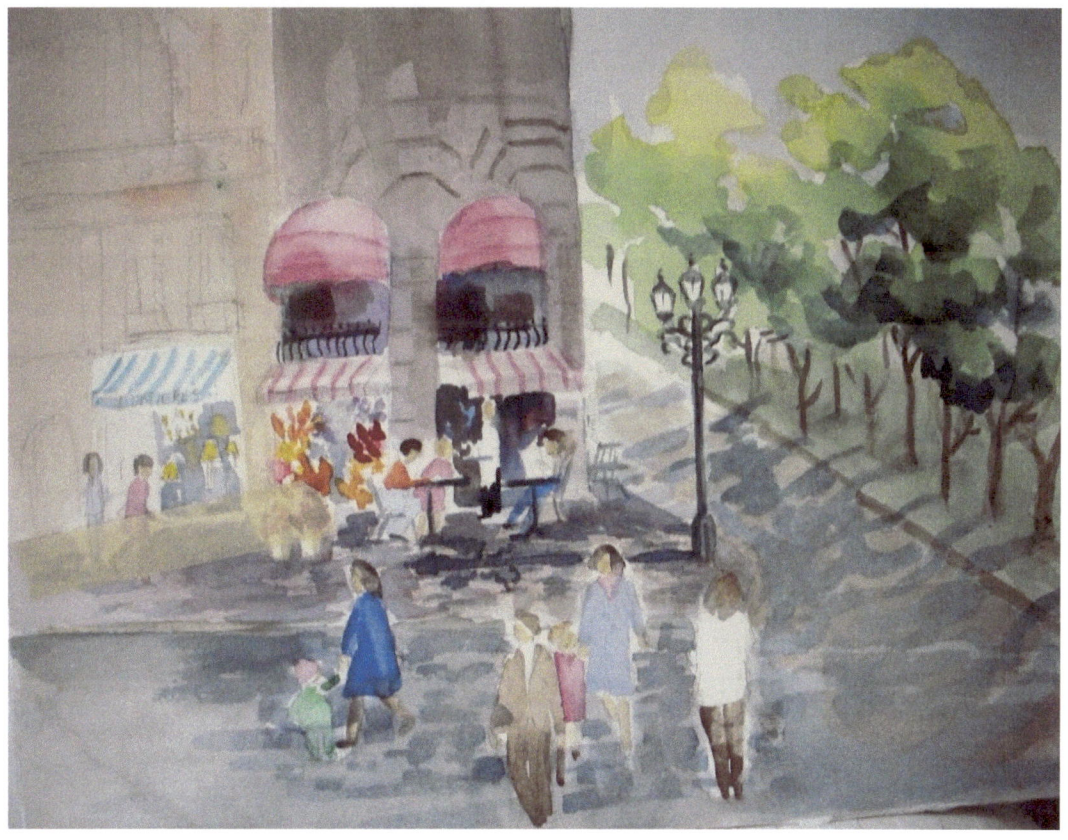

Monet's Impression

Monet's home

In Giverny

Is alive with spring flowers

And visitors soaking

In all the lovely

Gardens

That wind

In and out.

Over the pond

With weeping willows

Bowing down

To the artist's dream.

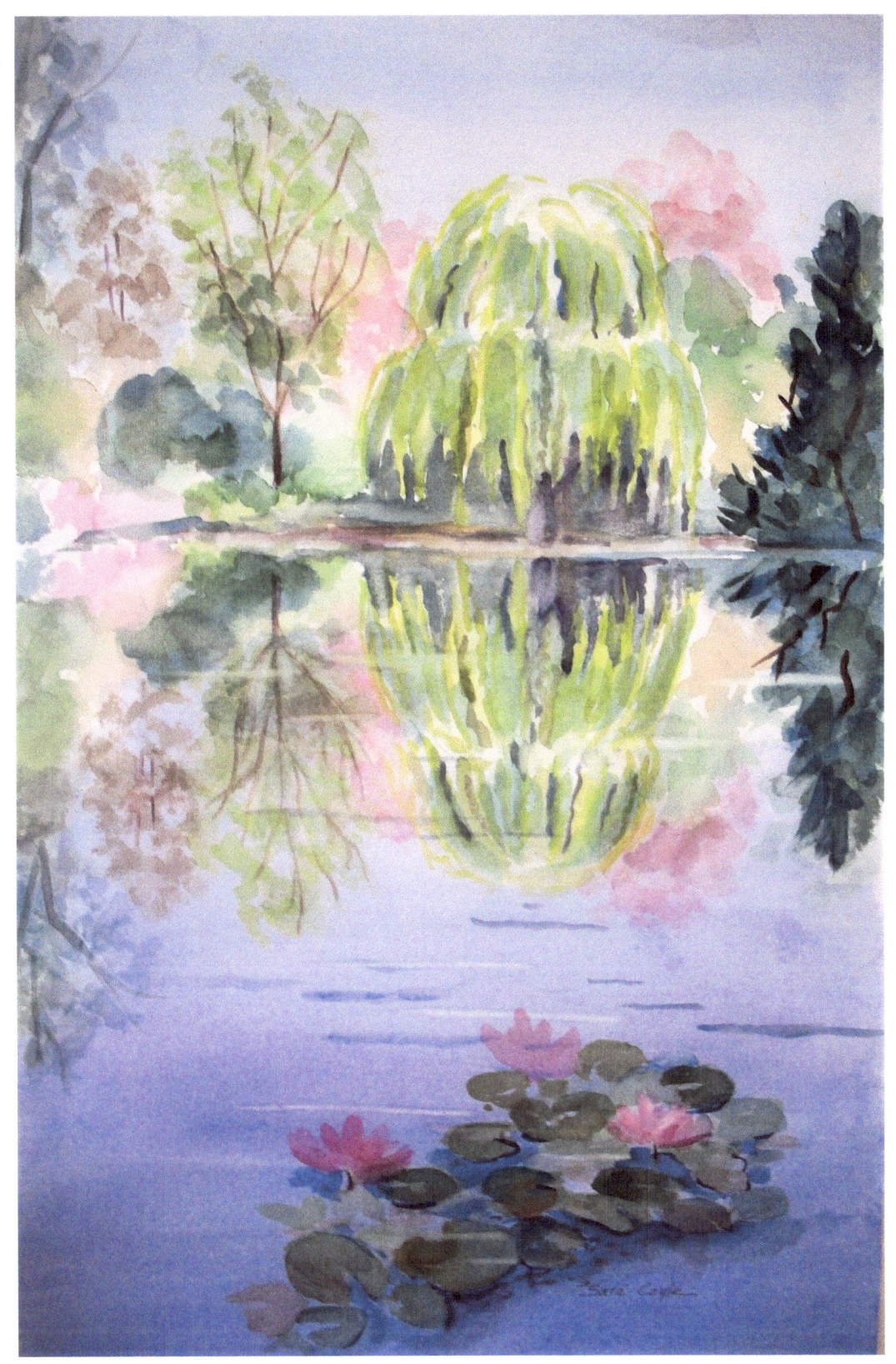

Tuscany

Rolling hills of Tuscany
Covered with hundreds of grape vines
Edged with rows of cypress.

Tall and dark- winding up the road
To the home and tasting room
Of the winery owners

The tourists enjoy these
Fine wines with laughter
And clinking glasses.
Cheers!

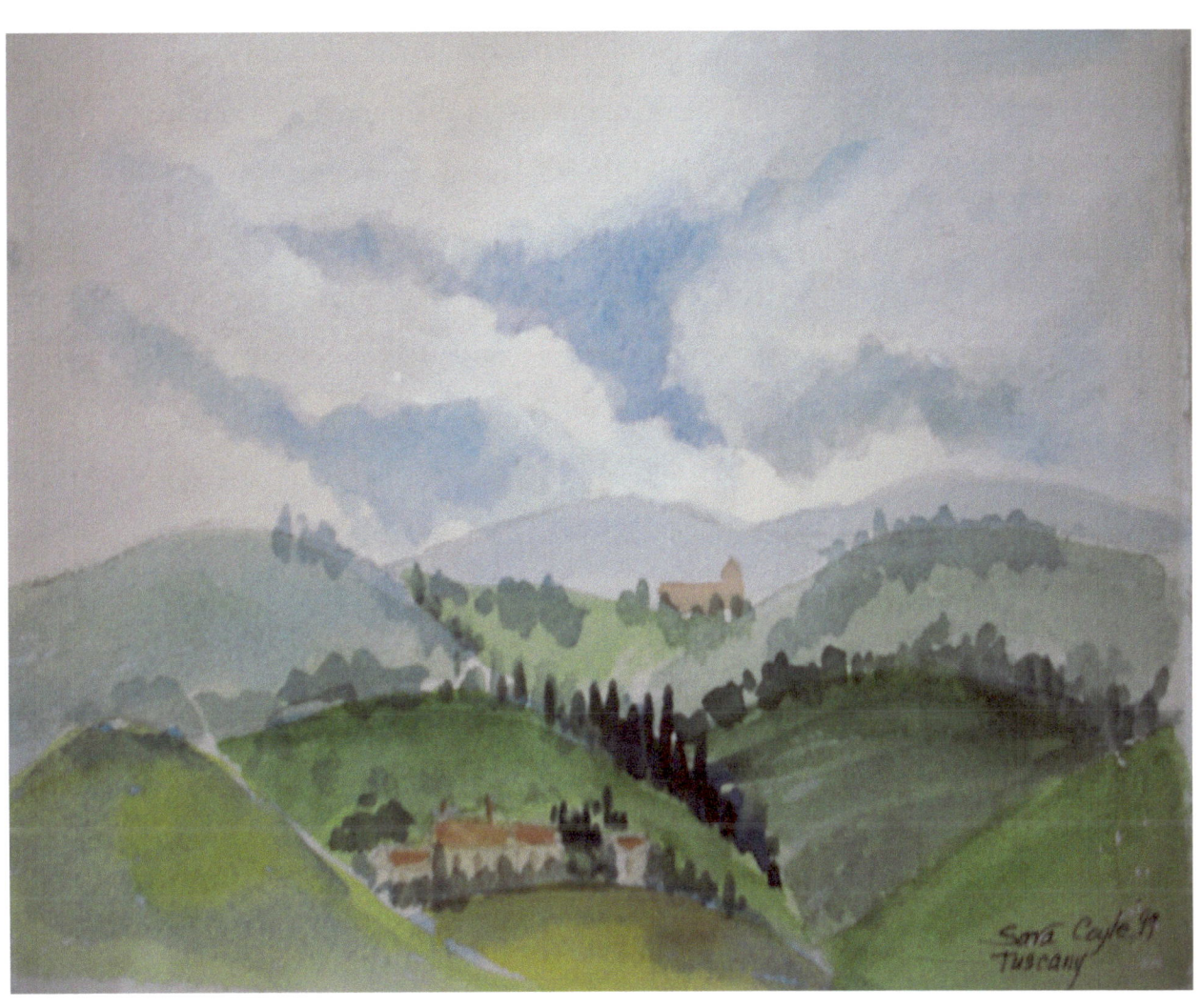

Roma

A city of antiquity

And the modern age,

Cell phone users rushing

By tall pillars of an ancient age

Weaving in and out of traffic

It's motor scooter congestions

While horses and buggies

Clomp slowly by with awe struck tourists.

Looking up

We see washing strung across buildings

Window to window

Having a dryer is still a luxury here.

So the modern age

Hasn't quite caught up.

Sitting outside at miniature tables

Covered with table clothes

The customers enjoy watching people

While eating.

Breathe in the air of ancient Rome.

Hear the music of Italy

Played on an accordion

and dream a roman opera.

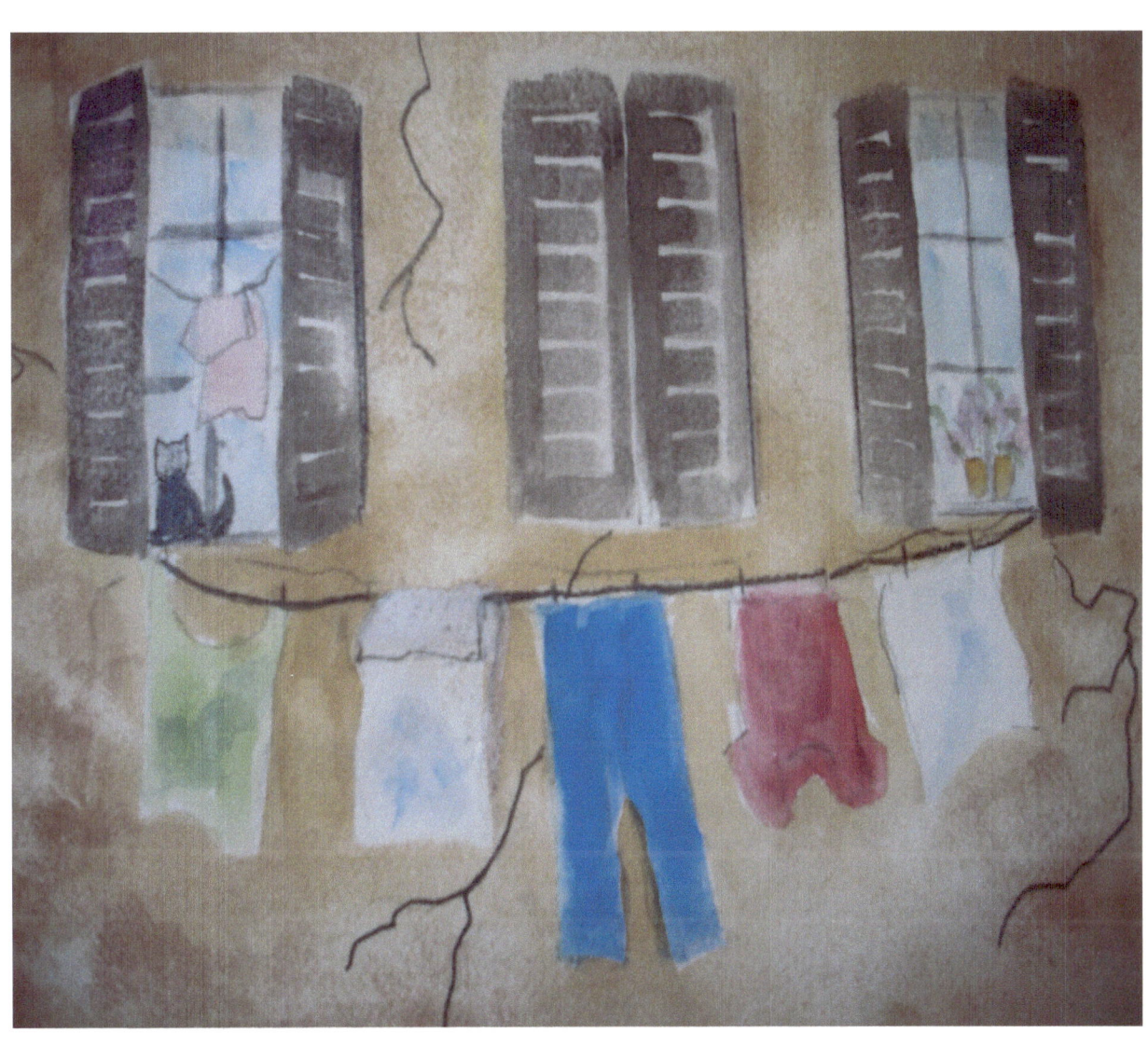

Color Everywhere

Walking through
Keukenhof Gardens in Holland
On a bright spring day was
An overwhelmingly beautiful
Experience.

The massive plantings of
tulips, hyacinths, daffodils and amaryllis
Were at their peak of bloom;
Bright color was everywhere

The ponds reflected the tall trees
And all this color around us.
It was a fairyland of beauty,
Brought about by the team
Effort of God and man.

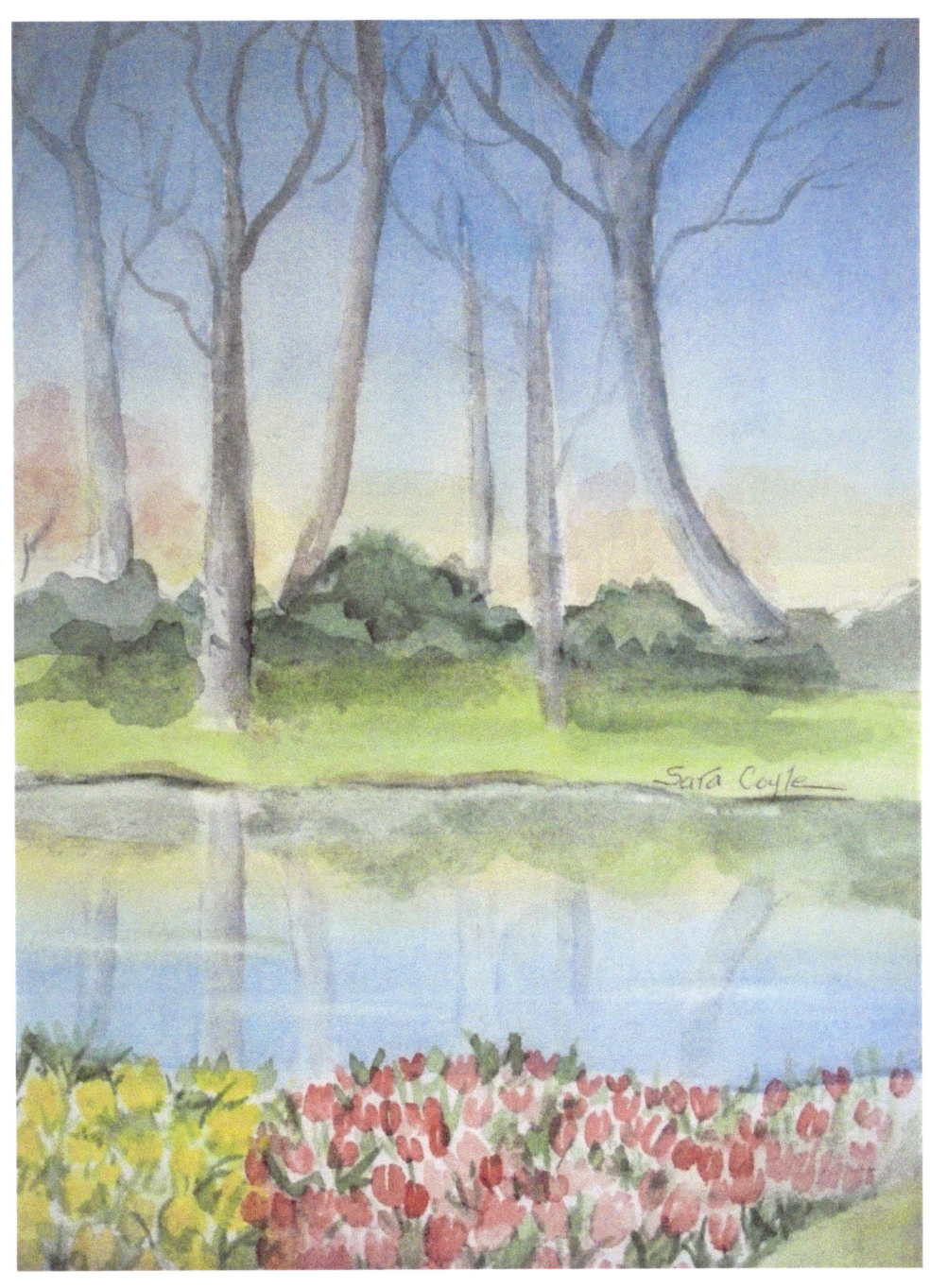

Sit in My Shade

We're home again
Sitting under the old
Oak Tree

The branches wind up and over
Under and around
Providing highways for
Squirrels, birds, and kids too.
Birds sing their tunes
High up in the trees.
Owls hoot the night away.
Opossum hang by their tails
Seeing the world upside down.

We sit in the shade
Of this ancient tree,
Feel the cool breeze,
And wonder at the tree's long life.

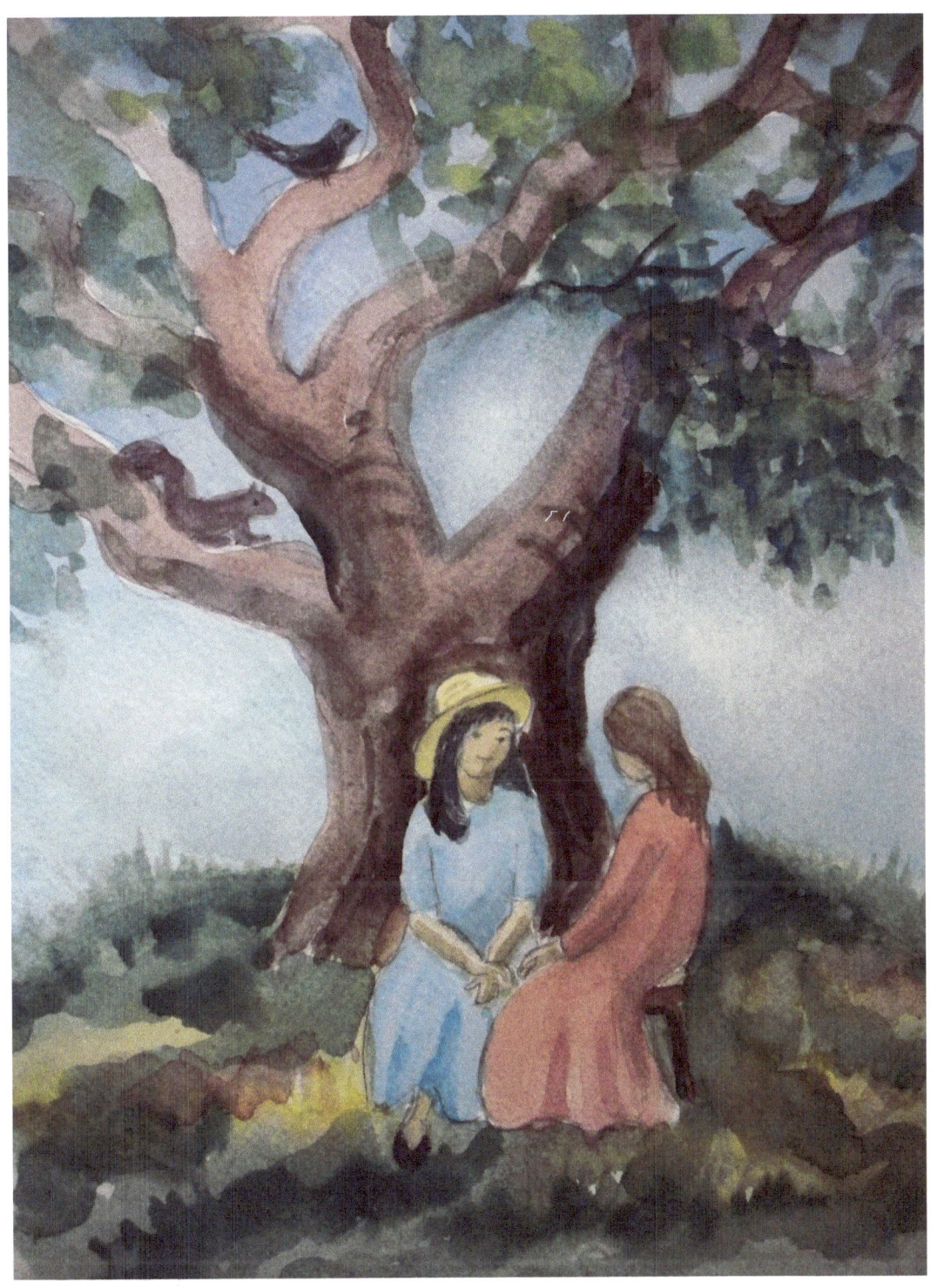

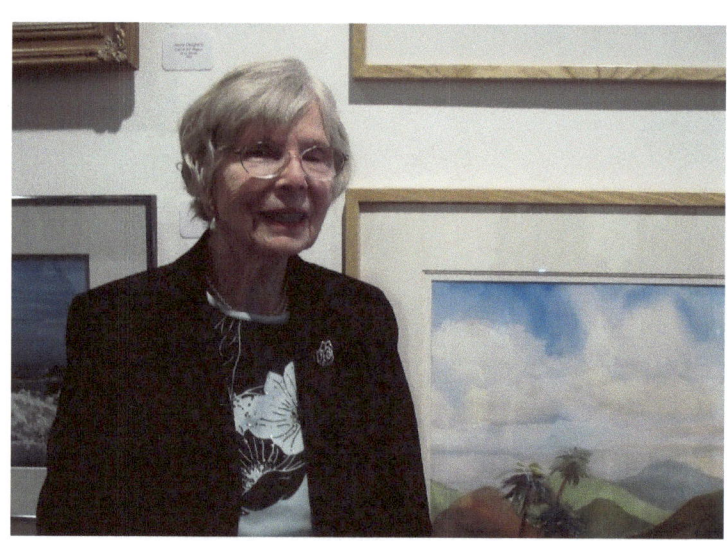

ABOUT THE AUTHOR

Sara's Paintings and Poetry is a collection of Watercolor paintings that Sara Painted on the trips she took near and far. She also wrote poems that tell stories about her travels. She lives in Southern California, continuing to paint and write and doing presentations of her original paintings and poetry.

www.ingramcontent.com/pod-product-compliance
Lightning Source LLC
Chambersburg PA
CBHW051200220526

45473CB00003B/842